ALWAYS
LEARNING

ALWAYS LEARNING

Lessons on Leveling Up,
from GameStop to Laura Mercier
and Beyond

GARY KUSIN

THREE WISE OLD OWLS PRESS

Three Wise Old Owls Press
2636 Farrington St.
Dallas, TX 75207

Hardcover ISBN: 979-8-9901085-0-9
Paperback ISBN: 979-8-9901085-1-6
Ebook ISBN: 979-8-9901085-2-3
Audiobook ISBN: 979-8-9901085-3-0

Jacket Design by Zoe Norvell | Interior Design: www.ineedabookinterior.com

For Melanie Kusin Rowe, my sister and the matriarch of a large and growing family, everyone's go-to for everything, powerhouse business leader, and spectacular, loving human on all levels. She is sorely missed.

Contents

AUTHOR'S NOTE

WE ARE ALL ON OUR own journeys. Some people have plotted out their journey from a very early age. Others, like me, started without a clue where they were headed. The old adage "If you don't know where you're going, any road will take you there" was especially true for me. Yet I managed to evolve and to make my own path. Along the way I have catalogued the stories that best describe that evolution from a young boy who had a hard time staying out of trouble to someone who had a successful career as an entrepreneur, CEO, and business turnaround specialist. Over time, others started asking me to share my stories, and I would hear back that my tales helped them on their own journeys.

This book is for anyone who feels uncertain about their journey and is looking for ways to help themselves along their way. I have learned it is less my successes that appeal to others but more the way I learned to make lemonade when I was being handed lemons. No one's path is perfect, but surprisingly few people realize that. Learning that everyone hits speed bumps is comforting, and it's good to know that there can be a way to work through tough situations and that we all have variations of the same issues.

The stories you will read here have been the richest in learnings for me, propelling my evolution during my journey. I believe they hold nuggets for people who may not know me or my story but are looking for lessons to help along their way. Mine is a story of learning, hard work, teaching, and evolution. I truly hope this book might provide helpful ideas readers can use on their own journeys.

INTRODUCTION

Seven Months, Seven Weeks, Seven Days, and Seven Words

TWO YEARS SPENT INTEGRATING KINKO'S into FedEx to become FedEx Office had come to a close, and I was feeling a general malaise. That was odd for me for an array of reasons, but most important was the fact that, for the first time in my life, I didn't need a job. Shouldn't I be happy? Hadn't I checked a box that few people get to check? So why wasn't I happy? I knew the issue had to be more complex than I could work through on my own. And I also knew, based on my corporate background, that there was a world of consultants who specialized in facilitated sessions working with families and businesses on issues from strategy to family dynamics. I thought a facilitated session could help me better understand my feelings.

My wife, Karleen, was having similar issues. Our youngest child was soon to head off to college, so after twenty-seven years of being a full-time mom, Karleen was going to become an empty nester. That knowledge was as destabilizing for her as my malaise was for me.

After a bunch of reference checks, we landed on a facilitator for a three-day session. The objective was to work through how we should think about our futures and create personal mission statements. The hope was that with a mission statement we would know best how to filter our potential paths forward. That session was groundbreaking for both of us. It was incredibly powerful, and it resulted in Karleen and me changing our personal trajectories.

To start, our facilitator gave us each a journal and asked us if we would suspend reality for a couple of days and just listen to her and believe what she was going to tell us. We agreed, and then she told us that we each only had seven months left to live. She asked us not to argue or ask for more information. It was very simple. We were going to die seven months hence. After that, she separated us into private spaces with our journals and asked us to spend several hours writing exactly how we intended to spend our last seven months on earth. We took our instructions seriously, and several hours later we sat down to compare notes. As you can imagine, such an exercise is very emotional, and if you take it seriously you do some deep soul-searching. We did, and each of us felt we captured how we would spend the seven months.

The next exercise was pretty shocking. Our facilitator started by apologizing because she had made a big mistake. The fact was, she told us, we did *not* have seven months to live, only seven weeks. She asked us if we would mind taking perhaps an hour and writing in our journal what we might do with only seven weeks to live. We dutifully did our work, and, not surprisingly, our lists were scaled down and more focused. After we reported our findings, she told us that it was actually seven days that we had to live. As you might imagine, our final journal entries were completely stripped down.

Our facilitator then asked us to write a couple of paragraphs about ourselves based on the evolution within our journals. She stressed that when you work down from seven months to seven weeks to seven days, you learn how to rank the priorities in your life and gain a deeper appreciation for what is most important and what is less important for you.

We each quickly completed the task. Our journals were full, and we had a good sense of what our priorities were. Our facilitator moved us through a process much like that in corporate mission statement work. We edited two paragraphs to one paragraph to three sentences to seven words. The process forces a person to use more descriptive words and drives them to focus on intentions.

Karleen came to grips with the fact that she had built her world around her family and had indeed raised a highly functioning and wonderful, creative, and loving family. But Caroline, our last child, was heading off to college, and Karleen would have no kids left at home. While she didn't know precisely what she wanted to do, she knew she needed to do something. The exercise helped Karleen crystalize in her mind that her future would feature a creative outlet for helping others. And it turned out that her dear friend Julie Tobolowsky was in the same situation, with her last child leaving home. Both of them share a joy of cooking, entertaining, and creating delicious gifts for teachers, friends, and family. By the time Karleen and Julie finished talking about the next step in their lives, a chocolate sauce and cookie business was born. Almost fifteen years later, the business has given each of them huge confidence in their capabilities and pride in what they have built. And what a beautiful way for both of them to express creativity and love! JK Chocolate, the company they started, is today a world-class cookie business with a large national reach and reputation based on its unique and delicious Microchip Cookies and chocolate sauces. Their products are one of the finest gifts in the United States.

The exercise helped me realize that, if you boil me down, I am about *learning* and *teaching*, in that order. I love learning new things and am very open and curious about the world around me. I understand the power of teaching and get my greatest satisfaction out of sharing with others in ways that could be helpful to them on their own journeys. There it was—learning and teaching—it was only three words, but I didn't have the energy at that point to stretch it to seven words!

From my earliest memories I enjoyed learning, though I kept my own counsel, even as a young child. I was raised in a home with a lot of rules, many about what children could do, but even more about what children could not do. And the rules were the rules, so there was no safe space where questions about rules or much else were acceptable from children. It was a home where, when a parent said, "Jump," the child said, "How high?" My resulting relationship with my parents was totally transactional. If I had a question or need, I raised it, and it was usually taken care of. But there weren't any emotional connections or expressions or discussions of love. Just getting through each day smoothly was the goal, and the only family focus was on book learning and school report cards. My real learnings came mostly by myself in my bedroom, pondering what I was being told in my home, among other things. I truly bristled then, as I do even now, when someone told me what to do. I wasn't buying what I was being told in my home, and telling me to do something without discussion became a huge trigger for me.

It was in my early adolescence, around eleven years old, that I first heard Darrell Royal, the head football coach of the University of Texas Longhorn team, say something that felt very important to me when he was questioned about a lucky outcome in a UT football game: "Luck is what happens when opportunity meets preparedness." That saying, especially the word *preparedness*, resonated with me—it made me believe that maybe I could actually influence the world around me. That perhaps the idea that "children should be seen and not heard" was incorrect, that children could have independent thoughts of their own.

That simple saying jump-started me on my way to a level of wellness I hadn't felt before. These insights converged at my first job in the family furniture store warehouse. It was my first "opportunity." Everything in life didn't have to be transactional. To have a warehouse full of bigger, older, and stronger people begin to respect me for the amount of work I could get done was an entirely new feeling, and I relished it! I worked harder and harder. I learned that if all else failed, you could find something that required competency, get competent, put in the hard work, and then reap the reward of respect gained.

Many of the pivotal points in my life have felt, at the start, seemingly disconnected, yet they ultimately became part of that pattern. With the Darrell Royal quote at the top of my mind, I evolved a refined sixth sense about opportunities. I developed a little radar in my head that would go on high alert when I heard or saw something new or different that resonated with me. What bound these disparate opportunities together, even when I was young, was that they required competence that could be gained through hard work and would result in respect if that work was successful. That is the mindset that allowed me to work several jobs simultaneously while in college to earn the tuition and spending money I needed. That mindset led me to do the work to get accepted into Harvard Business School (HBS), and from there start my career in the department-store sector—each step along the way was an opportunity that I recognized at the outset and then put in the work to turn it into reality. I cofounded two global brands. The first, named Babbage's at the start and later changed to GameStop, was the world's first video game retailer, and its first store opened at the dawn of the video game era. After that I cofounded Laura Mercier Cosmetics, which is today a major global cosmetics brand. I wasn't born with a passion for video games or cosmetics, but in both I saw opportunity that I could work and prepare for. I then participated in a roll-up in the serviced-office sector—think WeWork—before becoming CEO of Kinko's, turning that company from losing money into a $2.4 billion, highly profitable enterprise that was later acquired by FedEx. Each experience—mostly positive, some clearly negative—had a major impact on me, helping me further develop my own value system and beliefs about how business should operate in the world along with what traits were critical for a person to become successful in their career. One key element I learned early on was that so many people I met along the way didn't feel respected, much less seen as people. I had desperately yearned for respect, and I found it in a warehouse where most other team members weren't receiving the respect they deserved. From that point forward, I have put a premium on recognizing and respecting people from all walks of life. It is so easy to be respectful and interested in others, but in this day and age, it has become almost a forgotten trait in our society. During this time I also began to sense that recurring patterns were emerging from the variety of assignments early in my career. I started recognizing situations that I had experienced before. I kept my mind's aperture open in order to absorb the world around me. These experiences and my reactions to them evolved to form the core of my Leadership Principles, which, by the end of my career, were my business North Star. I will emphasize those points along the way as they crystalized for me.

My experience at Harvard Business School was life-changing for other reasons. When I was a student, HBS used the case study method to teach. Each class, rather than using textbooks, studied real stories from real companies. Each case described a company and a particular situation facing that company. It was our homework to read each case and then identify the issue or problem, discuss what might be the array of options available to deal with the issue, examine the strengths and weaknesses of each option, and then arrive at what we believed to be the proper course of action. For the first time in my life, I confirmed to myself that indeed there might be no single correct answer, but rather that several answers might work and that at the end of the day it is up to the participants to choose which course of action they believe should win the day. My world became much less black-and-white, as this method of learning flew in the face of the way I had been raised. Not only had I believed there was only ever one answer, but also I knew that I didn't get a vote on what that answer might be. College did nothing to disabuse me of that belief, but graduate school certainly did. The HBS classroom became my happy place and took a huge weight off my shoulders. I could think independently and believe that my thoughts had value. I realized that my brain could complement my brawn in the future as I continued gaining competency in the workplace along with the respect that competence engendered. Again, a far cry from what I was told as a child.

The void I had in understanding feelings, love, and intimacy was filled later by my wife, Karleen, our kids, Ben, Eric, Elizabeth, and Caroline, and now their spouses and our eleven grandkids. Each have helped and continue helping me learn how to become a more highly functioning adult and parent while discovering how to love and live happily. Not a small task!

My most important goal in writing this book is to pay it forward so that I can help readers on their own individual journeys. It is a way to mentor more broadly. Hopefully these stories help inspire some readers to recognize new opportunities in their own lives. Opportunities often come from surprising places and in unusual forms.

I seldom, if ever, use the word *should* in my mentoring, or, frankly, in my life. That is based on a handful of core beliefs:

1. Everyone carries their own baggage through their life. That baggage is full of every good and bad thing accumulated during their journeys. And these experiences create a prism through which each person views their world. These prisms are as individual as fingerprints. It is my hope that readers can view my stories through their own worldviews.

2. I have had very real advantages in my life. I became

acutely aware of the advantages as a teenager working that warehouse job. And there are so many other advantages that I encountered as I grew. Whatever pieces of my good fortune I can break off and hand to someone in other circumstances in order to help level the playing field, I am eager to do so, and if I accomplish some of that here, I will have succeeded.

3. I have had only a handful of special mentors in my life, but they have been exceptional. I know the value of such relationships, so I spend as much time as I can filling that role for others. In that context I am very consciously paying it forward.

4. Everyone, and I mean everyone, needs and wants help thinking about their own journeys. I certainly do! I have spent time with many CEOs talking about their personal issues and discussing their lives in depth. They walk around with the same worries and concerns as everyone else. If this book helps a reader sort out their issues in a new or different way, it will be a success.

5. While I believe that everyone should live their truth and their values, I also believe that over the course of a lifetime—with all the nicks, scars, joy, and pain that life brings—personal truth and values tend to change. I know mine have. There is a saying that you cannot remember not knowing what you now know. While I think that is generally true, I do know some things. Today I can cry with joy and gratitude when I see something heartwarming and with pain when I see wrongs. That was beyond my reach when I was younger. I believe that is just what happens as you gain a deeper appreciation for life.

It is in the spirit of learning and teaching that I selected these stories that track my evolution as a businessperson and the recurring patterns I observed that led to a set of leadership principles. These principles cut across industries and companies of all shapes and sizes, and they certainly will work for anyone.

Some of the stories are sad, some hilarious, some quite shocking, and some just plain weird! But there are mentoring lessons in virtually all of them, and as I look back it becomes easier for me to see how I have evolved into the person I am. I hope you will consider this a treasure hunt of sorts. See what lessons you can find for yourself from my evolution. If I succeed as a storytelling mentor, you will have a better feel for your own journey, understand what you can do to better prepare yourself for whatever comes your way, and learn to walk your truth with conviction that others have been there before you.

PART ONE

KEEPING MY OWN COUNSEL

High School Graduation

MY HIGH SCHOOL GRADUATION WAS in May of 1969. Texarkana Texas High School and the entire city were abuzz with excitement, having learned that the richest man in the world at that time, Ross Perot, a native of Texarkana, would be our commencement speaker. Earlier that spring, Ross had been featured on the cover of *Fortune*, which reported that he was the first ever billionaire in the United States. I was seventeen, and I was completely speechless to learn that because I was the student council president, I would be sitting squarely next to that billionaire on the stage during the ceremony. That May evening changed my life's trajectory, and as I look back on that experience, I find it fascinating in so many ways. Sitting in that chair on that stage was the unexpected culmination of a journey I had started six years earlier when I was eleven years old.

Before I sat on that stage next to Ross, my behavior was beginning to cause problems for my parents and teachers. I had received over a hundred swats from a paddle in seventh grade alone (I actually counted!) for various conduct infractions. I was an immature eleven-year-old looking for acceptance and love in all the wrong places and ways. Coach Maisel, my seventh grade math teacher, a retired baseball coach whose glory days had long ago passed, led the brigade of teachers, giving me the most swats for offering a middle finger salute when raising my hand, supposedly to answer a question, but really to get laughs—the laughs made me feel liked by my classmates. Thank goodness Coach Maisel's licks didn't hurt, but Coach Lee, the vibrant and intense young coach who was bent on producing tough young athletes, could bring the heat with his swats—his paddle had holes drilled in it to create welts on your backside. Once when Ms. Mitchell, my ninth grade English teacher, angrily told me in front of the class that if I acted out one more time, she would call my mother, I happily called out our phone number and told her my mother was at home if she would like to call her right then.

Big lesson finally learned that day—I had enough problems with my mother calling my father from time to time to come home from work to give me a whipping when I didn't deserve it. It was really dumb of me to challenge the authority of a teacher in her classroom. Those lashes hurt exceptionally, and I gradually began learning to never, and I mean *never*, reflect poorly on my parents' upbringing skills in front of other adults! Over the next year I gradually changed my behavior. But not before I played hooky one day and was chagrined to look out of the window of the city bus I was riding and lock eyes with my Uncle Sherman, who was driving next to the bus. He was fairly shocked to see me on a city bus in the middle of a school day. My parents and the principal were my welcome committee when I got back to F. Ben Pierce Junior High, and I got a few more swift swats from the principal while my parents looked on. This was one of my first opportunities to benefit from pattern recognition—but it hadn't registered for me yet. That's surprising to me today, as it was so obvious that there was a cause-and-effect relationship between conduct and corporal punishment. As the saying goes, "The view wasn't worth the climb," but that did not dawn on me at the time. It's clear why adolescence is so tough, or at least it was for me. I had a lot of maturing to do during this chapter of my life, and it took me longer to figure out these basic lessons than it did most other students.

My parents decided the best remedy for their juvenile-delinquent-in-training son was for me to work at the family furniture store warehouse every Saturday, holiday, and all summer days from that point forward until I left for college, and in the summers when I was back at home from college. At a minimum they figured it would keep me off the streets! My father would drop me at the warehouse each morning, and I would work until he swung by to pick me up on his way home each evening when the store closed. Our big warehouse, located blocks from the retail store, was hot in the summer and cold in the winter. I was the youngest person in the warehouse by far. I was also the only white person, joining anywhere from ten to twenty Black older teens and adults who did everything from unloading railroad boxcars of furniture directly shipped by train from the factories to emptying eighteen-wheelers at the dock and stocking the newly arrived inventory. In addition, this group packed delivery trucks with each day's deliveries and then drove routes within a fifty-mile radius of Texarkana, delivering furniture and laying floor coverings.

What my parents had no clue about was that a weight was lifted off my shoulders when I began working at the warehouse. At school I knew everyone and was friendly with most, but I never really had best friends or was part of a clique.

Over the next six years, until I left for the University of Texas, I was not just immersed in the world of furniture but also immersed in the Texarkana Black community. I was gradually accepted by the group, although I was the owner's son, which was cause for wariness, because I jumped to do the hard, sweaty work, learning all the tricks I could about furniture warehousing and delivery. And I was OK being the butt of jokes among the team. I was known as the grain of salt in the pepper shaker of the team, and I loved my uniqueness. One of the men, Julius Murphy, took me under his wing and is the person who taught me everything I needed to know to be helpful in the warehouse and on delivery trucks. Julius taught me all the tricks of leveraging your body and using the tools of the trade to move heavy, bulky weights. I was so thankful for his advice and leadership, and I worked hard to keep his approval. Julius was sixteen years old when his father brought him into Texas Furniture. As my father told the story, Julius's father guided Julius with his hand on the young man's neck, telling my father that if he hired Julius, he would become the best worker at the store. It turned out that Julius's father was correct! That was the same day I was born, and Dad had gone into the store to let everyone know of my arrival. That's how my father always knew the day Julius had started working at Texas Furniture. Julius and I later cemented our relationship in the other family business, the big local bowling center named Holiday Bowl, where we worked together after I graduated college. Julius was one of the strongest influences in my life, and I wouldn't be the person I am today without his imprint on me. It wasn't lost on me, even at that early age, that Julius was the most respected person in the warehouse due to his incredible competence.

I will come back to this period of my life again—as it was very formative—but for this story I will hit on only one thing, and that is the bigotry and racism this Black furniture warehouse team was exposed to every day. I was shocked to see the team so disrespected, and it made me angry. The worst infractions occurred on any delivery made to Fouke, Arkansas. Fouke was a small backwoods town twenty minutes south of Texarkana. I don't need to exaggerate this: Imagine a big billboard just outside of Fouke that had a demeaning artist's rendition of a young Black boy with a cane fishing pole slung over his shoulder, weighted down by a sack of clothes. The boy is looking back at the viewer as he is headed away from the town. The headline on the billboard said, "If you are colored, don't let the sun set on your head in Fouke, Arkansas." That billboard was outside of Fouke for many years. Multiply those episodes over decades, and you get a life full of indignities; some casual, some callous, and others so inhumane that I will never forget them. I have delivered furniture to homes where we were told I could come into the home but my Black partner on the delivery truck could not. It goes on and on—but for me the most amazing thing is the resilience the team had in the face of all the ugliness.

The warehouse was a safe haven for the entire team, including me. We would laugh and tease each other, eat our lunches and throw the bones (dominoes, though I could only watch because while I am quite good at math, I couldn't keep up with the scoring in dominoes—forget the math, knowing how to hit the worn-down chalk on a broken blackboard was tough all by itself). I would watch this group of guys I had grown to appreciate and would get furious that the world was such that they had to put up with that stuff. Those memories still haunt and infuriate me today.

When I say I was on the team, I mean that I had earned the right to be part of their group through my hard work. I could break down a boxcar of dining room furniture or an eighteen-wheeler of bedding. I could do it fast, right, and without complaining, usually all by myself. The competency I gained earned respect from the entire warehouse crew. It was my first ever true group of friends, and I loved it. While we ate our lunch, they would relate their various stories. I would listen, eating my regular lunch of a pickled egg with pickled bologna enjoyed with a tube of saltine crackers and RC Cola. If I was feeling flush, I would also grab a Moon Pie for dessert. On Saturdays when we were handed our pay envelopes, I would line up with my guys, proud in my work uniform that matched theirs, and get my six-pack of Colt 45 malt liquor tallboys and a pack of Kools or Tiparillo cigars. I am sure the store owner assumed I was of age to drink because of my work uniform and my sweaty brow as I tagged along with the group.

I learned later that Ross Perot was a fanatic about leadership. His motto was "Eagles don't flock, you have to find them one at a time." He only hired people at his company Electronic Data Systems (EDS) who had proven leadership skills, which Ross felt were always honed in military service. For me to be awarded a national leadership award while sitting next to him was like a slow pitch to Ross. He immediately liked me. The award I was being given at my commencement was a national Danforth Foundation *I Dare You* award for young leaders, and what earned me the surprise award was my role as student body president and the de minimis amount of racial flare-ups that occurred during that first year of full integration of Dunbar High School into Texas High School. The integration happened during my senior year in high school.

The late 1960s was an extremely violent period in US history: voting rights laws had been passed for the first time, as had laws about desegregation, and a large portion of white America was angry. Riots were breaking out all over the southern United States. During this period of desegregation, white folks would kill people just for mixing Black and white children in schools. The general consensus was that the same could possibly happen in Texarkana when Dunbar High School, with its long and storied history as part of the Texarkana Black community, was shuttered and the students were transferred to Texarkana Texas High School.

The turnover of employees in the Texas Furniture warehouse was such that I got to know easily over a hundred people during the six years I worked there. And all those people knew me. When the integration of Dunbar into Texas High School was announced, I asked some of my warehouse friends to introduce me to the student leaders at Dunbar. During the summer before senior year began I sat down with Harold Abney—the student council president of Dunbar—and several of the other student leaders to talk about what it would take to make the integration feel as seamless as it could for them and their classmates, especially during that first fall semester. I had pretty good credibility with most of them, based on the feedback from many in their community who knew me. The group of us broke bread at a little pool parlor near the warehouse that doubled as a grocery and food shop for Black workers in the area. I told some warehouse stories, and by the end of the session it became clear that while there was a long list of things that we could all work on, the most visible, early symbolic act of unity we could present would be hosting a soul band for the homecoming weekend dance. The Dunbar leaders felt that would be a good, if only symbolic, gesture, and if we could pull it off it would help ease early tensions and worries about students from Dunbar losing their identities in what had been the white high school. With the approval of Mr. McGuire, our principal, and based on my promise that it would be hugely helpful, we did invite the soul band, and it was a fine party. Of course, some white parents didn't allow their kids to attend, and there was pushback from others. For that and other initiatives we worked on, with varying amounts of success, I was surprised with the Danforth Foundation award.

A lifetime later, I am very sure that at a minimum Harold Abney should have been a corecipient, if not the outright recipient, of the Danforth Foundation award. He was the person who, though he had to give up his Dunbar High School student council president position, nevertheless didn't hold a grudge for the chain of events, and worked hard our entire senior year to be helpful in the integration process, receiving little recognition for his work in the effort to help ease tensions. Along the way he and I developed a nice, collegial relationship that carried past high school until his death. Today I do feel guilt about having received the award rather than Harold, and wish I had had the courage at the time to demand that the school make it right after the fact.

My relationship with Ross bridged the next fifteen years, and we developed a nice mentor and mentee relationship. After the commencement ceremony, Ross asked my parents if they would allow me to fly back to Dallas with him the next day, and of course they said yes. Ross took me on a Trans-Texas Airways commercial flight to Dallas— my first ever airplane flight—and I went with him to his house to drop off his luggage and then straight to his office, which was close by Love Field Airport. His office was the biggest office I had ever seen, with wall-to-wall plush pure-white carpet. It all made quite an impact on me. At Ross's request we called Harold Abney to get his reaction to Ross's commencement speech, which was positive according to Ross—I couldn't hear the other side of the phone call. Ross was always looking for feedback from the "front line," as he referred to it. He called me regularly while I was a student at the University of Texas to learn what the student body thought about the Vietnam War and other issues of the day. When he came to speak at Harvard Business School while I was a student there, he spotted me in the audience (mainly because I was sitting squarely in middle of the front row—an early example of what happens when opportunity meets preparedness!) and asked me to stay after his speech. We spent quality time there, again, and he probed me for HBS student attitudes about an array of issues.

Four years later when I moved to Dallas at age twenty-eight to take a senior merchant position at Sanger-Harris, the largest Dallas department store, I was among a few people the *Dallas Morning News* profiled as rising stars in the Dallas business community. My photo and an article were in a Sunday *Dallas Morning News*, and bright and early the following Monday morning Ross called my office at Sanger-Harris and asked me to come to his office. There he suggested to me that I shouldn't work for a big company, but rather should start my own company like he had. He promised me that if I ever did want to start a business, he would love to be my financial partner. Two years later Ross gave us the financial backing to start Babbage's!

I continue to marvel at how Ross, who had so many reasons to lapse in his interest in my career development, never stopped checking in on me from the time I sat next to him at my high school graduation. He has been a role model for me in how he followed up and followed through with me as I continued on my journey, despite the other demands on his time and attention.

The Payoff for Hard Work

FROM MY EARLIEST MEMORIES I was fiercely independent, probably to protect myself from being hurt. Through counseling as an adult, I learned that my independent streak was likely an outgrowth of my issues at home, which had led me to believe that only I could be counted on to take care of myself. And I learned over time that I was plenty capable of supporting myself in most ways.

Telling my parents I didn't need or want their money to pay for my college education, that I would provide the funds myself, is a clear example of my stubborn independent streak. I have never liked being beholden to anyone for any reason, and that drove my decision. I feared that their money might later be used as a blunt force instrument to demand some sort of behavior from me. I absolutely hated anyone telling me what to do—I wanted to believe I had agency. My parents didn't think I could actually pay for my own college expenses, but I worked every semester in college and always made enough money to both pay for college and to have walking around money to enjoy my college experience. My freshman year I washed dishes at Jester Dormitory for free meals—and got free meals without even working the second semester of that year because a boiler for the industrial kitchen dishwasher exploded when I was working nearby, scalding my arm and the right side of my body. A cafeteria manager brought me a document at the UT Health Center, where I had to spend the night. I signed without looking, learning later that it promised me free meals through the end of the school year if I promised to never sue them about the exploded boiler. I thought that was a great deal! I waited tables in my fraternity house my sophomore year for free meals there. I worked an overnight shift at a Circle K convenience store on the Drag and worked at a furniture store in Austin, Cabaniss-Brown Furniture, the entire time I was a student. My summer earnings from Texas Furniture always covered the balance of my cash needs.

I joined the ZBT fraternity at the University of Texas, which ended up being a hugely important part of my college experience, and remains so today. That group of guys—all Jewish—felt a lot like my warehouse community. I was immediately comfortable with them, and they let me be me, though not without the ribbing I had gotten used to in the warehouse. The fraternity members mostly hailed from Dallas and Houston, but some were from an array of small Texas towns and other large towns in the United States, from New Orleans to Memphis to Chicago. My deepest friendships today are with people from that group.

If luck is what happens when opportunity meets preparedness, then my biggest lesson during this period was that for me, hard work was how I prepared. It was something I could control and own the results of, and I was nothing if not energetic during that time in my life. I was pretty good at getting tough things done. My father reinforced that quality by never cutting me any slack if I was tired on a Saturday morning and wanted to sleep in. In fact, one summer day I drove two of our carpet installers to Lake of the Pines resort ninety minutes from Texarkana to lay carpet in a lake house. I went to make other deliveries in the area that I could deliver by myself and then returned to help them finish up the job. Once the job was done, my plan was to drive us all back to Texarkana. I had left my home that morning at the crack of dawn—maybe around 6:00 a.m.—to pick the guys up, as it was a long drive to Lake of the Pines. When I got back to the lake house around midafternoon, both of the carpet layers were passed out drunk on the floor and had done very little work. I roused them and learned that they had walked down to a nearby liquor store and had too much to drink when they returned. I called my father, told him the story, and asked what he would like me to do. He told me we had committed to getting the carpet laid that day, and I had to get the guys sobered up and oversee their work—the job had to be complete and done right before I could come back to Texarkana. Long story short, I helped them lay the carpet and we got it done (of course, wouldn't you know that house had a circular staircase in the entry hall—the trickiest installation job for a carpet layer!) and arrived back home after midnight that night. That had been an exhausting eighteen-plus-hour day. I tried to sleep in the next morning, but my father was in my room at 7:00 a.m. asking why I wasn't ready for work. I told him I was exhausted from the prior day. He said that that was yesterday and this was today and insisted I get dressed and get in the car. That was one of the best lessons I ever learned about hard work.

While the example of my father pushing me to work harder is a great, positive one, I also learned the hard way about what happens in the absence of hard work when preparing to meet an opportunity. I lost the eighth grade student council election, which I felt sure I would win, because I was outworked by my opponent. I hadn't abided by what Darrell Royal had said. I had *not* been prepared enough. My opponent was more prepared for the student council opportunity than me. That was a humbling lesson I have carried through the rest of my life. I decided then, at age thirteen, that while people could and would certainly outsmart me, they would never, ever again outwork me or be more prepared than me. That lesson has served me well ever since.

As I grew older, learning more about myself, I discovered that in addition to hard work, thinking creatively and outside the box was something that came naturally to me. Once HBS taught me that there could be multiple acceptable paths to take in most situations, I felt liberated to begin to think creatively about what alternative solutions might exist in various business situations. If there could be multiple solutions, then even if my thought didn't win the day, I would still get credit for having an interesting approach! The flip side of this is that if my idea was adopted and subsequently failed, I had no one to blame but myself. But I learned that owning my mistakes would be a requirement in any business, and I reasoned that all a person can do is reduce to irreducible the chances of failure and then live with the results.

I was also gradually learning to differentiate between which decisions were mine and which weren't. I knew to ask my father what he wanted me to do when the carpet installers were drunk on the job. He was the boss, and it was his store. However, on the other side of the coin, I believed that my choice of college was my own. It was, but this was an instance when my not wanting help or advice when I really needed some outside counsel blew up in my face. My parents asked me in the summer after I graduated high school what college I would be attending that fall. I told them the University of Texas, and they were surprised and said that they didn't know I had been accepted there. That stumped me. I hadn't bothered to inquire about the college admissions process, given my inclination to follow my own path. Talking to them, I learned for the first time that one had to apply to college and be accepted to that college before being permitted to attend. I had taken the SATs and somehow assumed that was all universities needed in order for someone to matriculate. Thank goodness that in 1969, all you needed to be automatically admitted to the University of Texas was to be a Texas resident in the top 10 percent of your high school class. But I didn't realize you still had to apply! It took me about a week to remedy my problem, and six weeks later I pulled away from my home in my Ford Mustang and drove to

Austin. I don't believe there is a college anywhere today that would admit someone who called them on July 1, asking to be admitted for the semester starting August 15, but it worked for me in 1969. It's not something I had thought about or intended to do, but as I drove down Potomac Avenue toward Interstate 30, by myself in the car, I let loose with the loudest primal scream. I had never done anything like that before. At first it scared even me, but it felt so cathartic! I was surprised by the scream but realized that I was happy to be leaving my life in Texarkana behind and going to a new place and into the next chapter of my life. That scream certainly speaks to how much tension had been building in me for so long during that time in my life.

Through my junior year I had absolutely no idea what I would do when I graduated from UT, and it weighed on me. I selected a new major each of my first four semesters, basing my choice on which class I made the highest grade in the prior semester since I didn't really have a passion for any classes I was taking. I thought that per-haps I would just go into politics since it had worked for me in high school and at UT. That all changed at the end of my junior year when my brother Michael got married in Wichita, Kansas. While I don't remember much about the weekend, the one thing I remember is that the trip changed my trajectory the same way sitting next to Ross Perot at my high school graduation had done. There were many people at the various wedding festivities over the several days we were in Kansas. What stood out most to me was that there was one man at the wedding whom everyone spoke about in hushed tones. The whispers told me that he was the richest man in Wichita and that he had an MBA from the Harvard Business School. By the end of the weekend, I had my new goals. The opportunity screamed to me. While I still didn't know exactly what I wanted to do after graduation, I was sure of two things. First, I wanted to go to the Harvard Business School, and second, I wanted to work exceedingly hard to create wealth like that person had. My internal bell had started ringing, perfectly on cue, letting me know that this was indeed a huge opportunity I had been preparing for. Lucky me!

HBS or Bust

I SET ABOUT ACHIEVING MY new goal first by determining I had to graduate from UT sooner rather than later so I could begin working to make enough money to afford HBS. That last summer before my senior year I worked the hardest I ever had. I will never forget my Monday through Friday summer work schedule. I figured I could make more money by working in Austin, so I had to piece together a schedule to earn serious money. I worked 10:00 a.m. to 2:00 p.m. daily as financial director of the UT student government to burnish my resume for HBS, 4:00 p.m. to 8:00 p.m. at Cabaniss-Brown Furniture, completing the migration of the inventory control system from a manual system to an IBM System/3 mainframe, and then from 11:00 p.m. to 7:00 a.m. at the Circle K convenience store near campus, mostly restocking the freezer units. Monday through Friday I took catnaps in the student union building and in my car.

I slept a lot on the weekends, mostly in my car, but I had a close friend, Jay Carter, who had given me a key to his fraternity house where some students lived over the summer when my fraternity house was locked down. Jay and I had become fast friends as Rowels in the Silver Spurs, an honorary service organization in charge of the care and feeding of Bevo, the UT mascot. Jay's key got me into the Kappa Alpha fraternity house for showers and sometimes to sleep on an empty bed when no one was around. It was quite the nomadic life, but it served its purpose of allowing me to make the money I knew I would need. I also knew I would move into an apartment when school started in August, so I just sucked it up and forged ahead.

To graduate in three and a half years instead of four required I take an overload of courses that first semester of my senior year, including one pass-fail class. I was going to graduate with a government major, so I decided I would take my pass-fail class in the UT Business School. The class was a computer programming course, and after I submitted my final exam, I learned I had failed the class! I went into the professor's office frantic and told him I was a government major and thought it would be interesting to take his course since I had not taken any business school classes at UT. I told him that I needed that grade to be a pass so I could graduate and begin earning money. He asked what I was going to do after graduation, and I told him I didn't know but would probably go into politics, fearing that if he knew I was applying to HBS, he would not change my fail to a pass. After a few moments of silence, he told me that if I promised to never go into the business world, he would change my grade from a fail to a pass. My suspicion he might not pass me if he knew I was applying to HBS was correct. I immediately promised I would be a public service guy, and he changed my grade. I graduated in December of 1972, after three and a half years at UT. When I gave the commencement speech at the University of Texas McCombs School of Business many years later, I opened my speech with this story. The graduates howled and cheered, and the administrators remained fairly stoic. I guess that while that conversation with the professor was painful at the time, it was certainly worth it, as it made a great story!

Now that I had completed my first step, graduating early from UT, I needed to move on to completing the HBS application and working hard enough to make the money to pay my way once I was accepted. I had read everything I could get my hands on about HBS and felt I was quite qualified: I had worked in the furniture warehouse starting at an early age, I had worked my way through UT, and I had some nice leadership honors there due to my heavy involvement in many leadership and student government activities along with leadership roles in Austin charitable organizations and the ZBT social fraternity. I also had three great references for my application in Margaret Berry, dean of students at UT, Professor Norm Frohlich, my major UT government professor, and Hiram Brown, owner of Cabaniss-Brown Furniture, where I had worked my entire time in Austin.

I submitted my application and immediately got busy trying to make all the money I could to help pay for HBS. I started by computerizing the inventory management and warehouse operations at Texas Furniture with what I had learned in my time in Austin at Cabaniss-Brown Furniture. I completed that task very quickly and was looking for something else to do until I could start at HBS. Holiday Bowl was the best opportunity that presented itself. My father and his brother-in-law Leo Bishkin had opened Holiday Bowl in the mid-1950s as an investment, and it had done well over the years. Since I was trying to make money while marking time until I could start at HBS, I spent my evenings at Holiday Bowl, mostly hanging out with Julius Murphy, who kept all the bowling equipment working in both the back and the front of Holiday Bowl during his evenings, in addition to his work at Texas Furniture. After a month or so spent at Holiday Bowl, I felt I could manage the business better than the current manager and asked my father and Uncle Leo if they would let me become manager. They were happy for me to begin that position.

And then the letter arrived from Harvard Business School. I was shocked to learn that while they accepted me for admission, the letter said they wanted me to work for two full years more before matriculating. I was infuriated! Had they not read my application? Did they not know I had worked since I was eleven at Texas Furniture? Did they not know I worked three jobs in Austin and was financial director of the student government? I was stunned, and the prospect of waiting an extra two years was completely unpalatable. I made a decision to get in the car, drive to Boston, Massachusetts, and find the director of admissions, Rand Neyland, who had signed my admission letter, and let him know he had made a mistake by deferring me for two years. It had to be a mistake, right?

Fierce Independence Meets HBS Admissions

I HAD NEVER BEEN EAST of the Mississippi. By this time, I had traded my Mustang for a blue Opel GT. It was very cool for motoring around Austin and for going back and forth to Texarkana, but it was not suited for cross-country travel. I bought a road atlas, borrowed my father's yellow Plymouth Satellite, and drove directly to Boston. I found the campus, parked, and—sporting my best white socks, jeans, and loafers—went into the admissions building and found Rand Neyland's office. When he came out to see me, I showed him the letter and told him I thought a mistake had been made. He looked at the letter and laughed and said I had been accepted, so he was confused about what the mistake might be. I said that requiring me to work for two more years after all my accumulated work experience felt wrong, and I wondered if they had read my application. He assured me they had, but that they required two years of post-college work experience with very few exceptions. I told him I still felt that was wrong, and he asked me to wait in a conference room while he could invite some other people in his group to come meet me.

Soon I was sitting at a big conference table with a bunch of men in suits staring at me. With all the courage I could muster, I restated my issue. They asked me some questions, and then Rand asked me what I was doing for work since I had graduated early. I told the group how I had computerized the inventory control and management function at the family furniture store and how I had recently become the manager of the family bowling center in Texarkana. In what I thought was a fair compromise, since it was becoming obvious that they weren't going to allow me into HBS straight from college, Rand said I should send him a current income statement from Holiday Bowl showing the revenues, costs, and profit from the twelve months prior to my start date. And then in twelve months I should send them the income statement from my first year as manager, and if results showed "strong improvement" under my leadership, HBS would admit me after only twelve months' work, something they said would be out of the ordinary. I stuck my hand out to shake his and told him we had a deal. The group kind of cheered and wished me good luck, and off I drove halfway back across America to Texarkana, feeling successful and proud of myself while also feeling dread wondering how I was going to move the needle at Holiday Bowl. To give you a preview, I became one of a small number of HBS students who only worked for one year after earning their undergraduate degree prior to starting classes at HBS. I actually generated more profits in my twelve months at Holiday Bowl than had been total revenues in the twelve months prior to me starting as manager.

How Holiday Bowl Sealed the Deal

THE BOWLING BUSINESS IS VERY simple. There are very high fixed costs to open a bowling center, meaning you spend a lot of money on machines, lanes, and equipment to open for business, but there are very low variable costs. Variable costs are the costs associated with people actually bowling. At Holiday Bowl you really only needed one person in the back of the bowling center at the ready to fix machines if they break down when people are bowling and one person on the front counter handing out bowling shoes to people who want to rent shoes, whether only one lane is operating or all thirty lanes are going full tilt. Clearly there was a lot of money to be made from keeping thirty lanes fully operating rather than fewer. The other bowling revenue items were very high margin. Imagine Holiday Bowl paying eight dollars wholesale for a pair of new bowling shoes and then charging fifty cents each time someone wanted to rent those shoes to bowl. After a pair was rented sixteen times, you had all your money back. We usually rented a pair of bowling shoes hundreds of times before destroying them. Some business model!

There is recreational bowling, and there is league bowling. Recreational bowling is when a family or a group of friends walks in to bowl. League bowling is when a large group of people bowls regularly every week on teams against other teams. The obvious objective, then, is to fill as many lanes as you can each day with leagues because it is a steady stream of weekly revenues with very low cost. I realized that most leagues were teams of employees at local companies. It seemed that the easiest thing I could do would be to convince local businesses to allow their employees to form their own bowling leagues—I would pitch that it would be fun and good for company morale. I made a list of the biggest companies in Texarkana and started visiting them one at a time, promising six weeks of free group bowling lessons. I would teach everyone how to bowl, and in the seventh week they would form their own company league, committing to twenty-week league seasons of regular weekly bowling. It turned out there was considerable demand for bowling, and that demand had only needed to be tapped by someone to give the companies the road map to starting their own leagues. Holiday Bowl went from fifteen of the thirty lanes being used each evening for leagues to all thirty lanes taken every night with two shifts of bowlers each night except Saturday nights. That means we filled thirty lanes at 6:00 p.m. and then filled all thirty lanes again at 9:00 p.m. with Texarkana-area company leagues. Holiday Bowl became a major part of the social scene in Texarkana, and our restaurant and bar service exploded, along with our pool room and upright arcade business. Revenues and profitability soared, and I made good money for HBS tuition, just not enough! I was beginning to see a pattern linking all the hard work and the results. But for the first time, my hard work was using my head rather than my muscles. I liked it, and I liked the respect I received from my father and Uncle Leo as I blew away any historic results they had in the past at the bowling center. There it was again—gaining competence resulted in respect. On the flip side of that, I have been sensitive to the idea of pay for performance ever since. For $200,000 of profit in a single year I received a $900 bonus! Ugh!

During the time I spent at Holiday Bowl, I cemented my relationship with Julius. Not only had he taught me the furniture business, he then taught me the bowling business. Plus, Julius and I bowled regularly together, shot pool together, played pinball together, ate meals together, and discussed our worlds together. We also became the first integrated two-man team in the Holiday Bowl scratch league, the league for the best bowlers at Holiday Bowl. Julius was loved by everyone at Holiday Bowl, so it was an easy thing to pull off, but it was a first in Texarkana and was very gratifying for both of us. And as good a bowler as I was, Julius was always a bit better. Don't think all these years since have made him forget that! He was and remains today one of my dearest lifelong friends.

Key Lessons

PART 1

Seize Transformative Moments:
Life-changing encounters, such as meeting influential figures, can redirect your path. Embrace these moments and the new trajectories they offer.

Accountability and Reflection:
Recognize the value of self-reflection and accountability for your actions, as these are crucial steps toward maturity and personal growth.

Diligence and Commitment:
Understand that a consistent work ethic and dedication are
keys to earning respect and achieving long-term success.

Understand the Impact of Prejudice:
Commit to recognizing when you are part of the
problem and become part of the change. Advocate for
equality and respect.

Build Lasting Relationships:
Cultivate meaningful relationships through shared
experiences and mutual respect. These bonds can become
a source of strength and support.

Pursue Education Passionately:
Education is a journey that requires passion and effort.
Take charge of your learning path with enthusiasm and
determination.

Financial Independence:
Strive for financial independence as a foundation for making
autonomous life choices. It affords you the freedom to make
decisions based on your values, not your needs.

Confront Challenges Head-On:
Tackle life's obstacles with courage. Whether it's addressing
personal flaws or societal injustices, facing challenges
directly fosters resilience.

Harness the Power of Community:
Engage with and contribute to your community. Whether
it's a fraternity or sorority, workplace, or neighborhood,
communal ties can propel you forward.

Embrace Adaptability:

Be adaptable in the face of change. Flexibility in thought and action is essential to navigate life's unpredictable nature.

Strategic Preparation:

Understand the importance of strategic preparation for life's opportunities. Whether in education or career, being well prepared is often the bedrock of success.

PART TWO

GATHERING EXPERIENCES

Socrates Meets Pattern Recognition

TALK ABOUT EXPANDING YOUR HORIZONS! Going to Boston to start a two-year stint on the Harvard Business School campus was about as far afield as a young person from Texarkana could get! The weather was much colder than in Texas, and most buildings remained from a time before Texarkana even existed. It was crazy, and all my senses were piqued.

I was so excited for the two years of school, and the campus life did not disappoint me. I was very prepared for case studies since all the books about HBS went into great detail about the case study method. What I had not properly appreciated on my arrival at HBS was the Socratic method of teaching employed at HBS. The Socratic method is essentially a dialogue between teacher and students, initiated by the teacher's probing questions of the students during class discussion, in a concerted effort to explore and validate (or not!) the underlying beliefs that shape the students' views. I *loved* this process. The main concept behind it is that there may be many answers to a single question, or at HBS to a case study. That was very liberating for me, as

I grew up thinking it was a binary world—everything was either right or wrong. This method of teaching quickly communicated that there could be many answers, some perhaps better than others, but many options nevertheless. Since I am much better in conversations, this teaching method gave me permission to represent and debate my point of view during classes. I didn't need to memorize things in books and regurgitate them on tests. I got to read, think, internalize, and then debate my points of view. It was so enjoyable that I have used the Socratic method from HBS over the course of my career and still do in my mentoring today. I think it is the best way to teach and to learn. And it maximized my learning at HBS.

We studied over seven hundred cases during our two years at HBS. The cases were generally all written in the same format: Some discussion of what or why the CEO of a company was worried. Then some paragraphs about the CEO's perceived issue, competitors, and the team reporting to the CEO. There were lots of tables with numbers in the back of each case. So once the question posed by the case was understood, the reader would dive into the data to parse it for answers or at least further questions. The surprise for me was how quickly I adapted to the case study method. It became the most powerful example of pattern recognition I had seen. After all, it only took a hundred swats of a paddle in seventh grade to realize a pattern. Imagine studying seven hundred cases over two school years! I realized I was learning a ton very quickly, including how parsing for patterns is powerful. It does not yield an answer with 100 percent accuracy, but it definitely gives a leg up in working toward the best option in a given situation. I had been unknowingly preparing for this case study approach for as long as I could remember. I had been keeping my own counsel since I was young, absorbing a fact set and then watching to see how it played out. I had gotten pretty good over the years at the treasure-hunt approach of parsing for patterns. HBS was a treasure trove of patterns, though each functional area was different. For instance, in the finance area you should always jump straight to financial information to find the issue—after all, you were in a finance class! While in marketing you could be sure the real issue was somewhere in the product, customer, pricing, promotional, or channel areas. And with a case in human resources, it was always about how employees were managed, or sometimes mismanaged.

I especially enjoyed learning about things that appeared counterintuitive until they were thought about more deeply. Two great examples were the Smucker's Ketchup case and the Cuisinart case. Both companies were faced with a seemingly intractable, maddening, unanticipated situation. The issues in both cases appeared to be counterintuitive. Finding the patterns was a bit of hide and seek. First, obviously because we were in a marketing class, the issue was a marketing issue. That alone lowered the array of potential topics and solutions available. Could it be a pricing issue, a product issue, or a promotional issue? These companies, and thus, these case studies, came to teach something new and different about marketing each day. And as is true in most business cases, being armed with the best information leads to a better-informed thought process. That isn't to be confused with success. Sometimes the result is learning with a high degree of precision that the product failed.

Smucker's had created a huge business based on the highest-quality jams and jellies. They felt an interesting adjacent business would be ketchup. After all, what could be better than creating the highest-quality ketchup to match their other high-quality products? The result was both the highest-quality ketchup on the market and an enormous failure for Smucker's! How could that be? Why didn't people like it? The company learned later that the bottom line was that people use ketchup to make whatever they are eating taste like ketchup. Eggs. Hot dogs. You name it. If a person is adding ketchup, it is to make the food taste like ketchup. Smucker's ketchup, while made of great ingredients, didn't taste like regular ketchup, so people didn't like it. The high-quality ingredients created a taste profile that was slightly different from that of the typical ketchups on the market. Smucker's had done customer focus groups but never to get at a taste profile, which was a big miss for the company marketers. The Smucker's focus group objective was to understand whether the customers would try a new ketchup from Smucker's. Actual taste had not been part of the original work plan. And, frankly, it wasn't even obvious to ketchup customers that they liked ketchup because it made whatever they were eating taste like ketchup. With this new information, since it pretty much killed the notion of Smucker's having a competitive edge because of the quality of their ketchup, Smucker's dropped the product. I have used that story at opportune times throughout my career. Ditto the other case study, Cuisinart.

Cuisinart had built the best food processor on the market by any measure. The machine simply ground up whatever was in it better than any other food processor. But they couldn't give them away. There were so many food processors on the market that Cuisinart couldn't break through all the noise in the marketplace. Then, in a first for any company with a failing product, they decided to *raise* the price! And then raise it again and again. Pretty soon they had the most expensive food processor on the market, and since it was such a unique high-quality product with results customers could see, owning a Cuisinart became a status symbol. People not only paid the ridiculously high new price of $150 (in the mid-1970s), Cuisinart couldn't even keep up with demand. By 1977 it became the best-selling and highest-priced home appliance in history.

So here were two very different cases, one a big failure and the other a soaring success—but with the same patterns. Both were marketing issues (of course, we were in a marketing class!) That dramatically narrowed down where I looked for solutions. And based on the specific area of marketing we were studying, I knew the first places to look were the five *P*'s of marketing: product, promotion, pricing, place, and people. Sure enough, Smucker's was a product issue and Cuisinart was a pricing issue. While this all seems simple enough, these lessons and approaches have withstood the test of time for me.

To make the learning even more enjoyable, sometimes the key players in the actual company covered in the case study would slip into our classroom unannounced, sit at the back of the classroom, and then at the end of class be introduced and tell us what was actually done in the particular instance of the case, followed with their description of how it worked out for them.

There were so many things to learn for me at HBS, and the biggest was diagnostic ability. In the real business world, you face new and different problems daily. Business isn't broken down as neatly as graduate school classes might be, so it is a search to find exactly where the problem resides. But patterns are real. I learned that simply by asking questions in a Socratic way, I could get to an answer that fit a pattern I had learned at HBS. Define the problem first, being very disciplined in the approach to identifying and articulating that problem. Then do a root-cause analysis to understand what precisely went wrong to bring focus to the issue. Work to define a set of alternatives to correct the issue. Sort through the strengths and weaknesses of each alternative, and then select the alternative that appears to have the best potential for success. This questioning and searching for patterns was a construct that has helped me mightily in business.

On the Bayou

SURPRISINGLY, THE SUMMER BETWEEN MY first and second years at HBS was very special. As usual, I desperately needed money, so I went to the placement office and looked for which employers recruiting were paying the most for summer interns. One company stood out—Security Industrial Insurance Company, based in Donaldsonville, Louisiana. The company was offering $2,500 a month for work as an intern for the owner during the summer. I could barely spell insurance, but I had never made that much money in a month either, so I applied and landed the position.

The man who owned the company was a larger-than-life character! His name was E. J. Ourso (OOS-oh!), and he was as Cajun as he could be, living in a small town in the bayou country between Baton Rouge and New Orleans. As a child, E. J. sold live chickens door-to-door, and as he got older he started selling a particular kind of burial insurance called debit insurance. Debit insurance guarantees a person a particular type of funeral, all expenses paid, when the person dies, regardless of how much money the person had paid for that insurance policy at the time of death. In the mid-1970s, their advertising message was that if you paid ten cents a week for your insurance, when you died you would be guaranteed a $200 funeral. And they would illustrate examples in their advertising of a real person who might have paid their first ten cents at age one hundred, died the next day, and then sure enough was given a $200 funeral.

E. J.'s company had over five hundred people selling this insurance throughout Louisiana, and it was hugely successful. In addition to the insurance, they also owned the funeral homes, the cemeteries, and the florists used for funerals. They were completely vertically integrated, meaning they had every part of the customer life cycle (or should I say death cycle) covered to make the highest profit margins.

E. J. was so colorful! He was maybe five feet, ten inches tall and easily weighed three hundred pounds, likely much more. And he was absolutely beloved by his employees. He would always wear a seersucker suit and a straw fedora. And he could, as he would often say, dance a jig at a funeral! How he loved his Harvard MBAs each summer. His pronunciation of MBA was M-uh, B-uh, A-uh. No matter what we had done during each week, every Friday morning he would make the three of us sit in a row with our hand-pulled adding machines and compute his personal net worth. And every Friday he would put his very big hands around my very scrawny neck while I was computing and bellow, "What have you done so far this week to make me *mo' money?*" I thought he was one of the funniest characters I had ever met, and I teased him right back, which sometimes caused others to gasp, or cringe and look away. He was clearly playful, but others always deferred to him because of his wealth, I guess.

E. J. was just so much fun to work for, and because he liked my teasing, he quickly made me his designated driver. As his driver for that summer, I would take him everywhere, our Chevrolet tilting in his direction every time he got in the car. In the process I met people like the Louisiana governor Edwin Edwards and Senators Russell Long and J. Bennett Johnston in private rooms in New Orleans restaurants like Antoine's or Galatoire's. I would wait outside the door of the private dining room until the meal was finished, but I was always introduced with "this is my Hahvuhd M-uh, B-uh, A-uh drive-uh." I never knew what went on behind the closed doors and wished I did, but I figured it was best that I didn't!

E. J. and his wife, Ms. Marjorie, would call Karleen and me years later whenever they were in San Francisco and take us out to dinner. Today the business school at Louisiana State University is named the E. J. Ourso College of Business. One last E. J. story: the way he managed the steady flow of HBS students to Donaldsonville each summer was to have the prior year's interns select the new interns for the following year. And E. J., with his signature lavish graciousness, allowed us to host the new recruits we had selected for a dinner in the nicest, most expensive restaurant in Boston once they all signed on. In 1976 that restaurant was Locke-Ober, and I coordinated all the details. We had a great evening, and about a week later I got a call from E. J. saying, "Gary, I gave you an unlimited budget for your dinner with the new recruits, and for the first time since I started doing this, you actually went over my budget!" I was silent for a minute, and then he started belly laughing in his inimitable way and said, "Just teasing. I am really going to miss you!"

E. J. was one of a kind! And I miss him also. He was my first example and role model for a superb CEO. He had so many qualities of what became my Leadership Principles. Most importantly, every person in his company very clearly understood the company vision and rallied around it always. There was such alignment across the company with E. J.'s vision: selling a product that ensured that at life's end a person would have a very respectable and dignified funeral regardless of their financial circumstances. It gave customers comfort and peace about their end of life. And the employees of his firm all shared a commitment to that mission. Finally, E. J. not only made work fun by hosting annual conventions for the sales force in places they could never afford to go to on their own, but had incentive systems that allowed high performers to make very good livings, beyond what they ever could have dreamed. And to top it off, he did do things like wear a hula skirt and dance a jig at a company meeting after a year of terrific results. I learned so much from him, not just about performance and wealth, but about how to manage people and the value of treating people with respect and dignity. While I certainly had other examples later in my career of the impact of a leader lacking those critical qualities, it was wonderful that early in my career I got such a superb example of what could be.

The HBS Opportunity Payoff

LEAVING MY BROTHER'S WEDDING WITH my two new goals of attending HBS and then finding a way to make real money paid off toward the end of my second year in graduate school. Everyone was interviewing all over the world, and the top students were getting annual compensation offers from $23,000 to $27,000 from Wall Street firms, consulting firms, and the big accounting firms. I couldn't even think about what I wanted to do when I graduated. I was totally afloat in a sea of options, none of which seemed appealing to me even though the starting salaries were very high for that time period. I took a class in retailing thinking maybe I could learn something of interest for my father, even though I had no interest in working at the furniture store. The retailing class was very small, maybe twenty-five students total, as retailing wasn't really an in-favor industry at HBS during my time there.

One day the CEO of the May Company, Dave Farrell, came to speak to our retailing class. The May Company was the second largest department-store company in the United States, second only to Federated Department Stores in size. Since I was acutely aware of what offers my friends were receiving, I started asking Mr. Farrell what an organization chart looked like for his company, where we might start on his chart if we joined the May Company, and what our starting salary might be. Then I pressed him on how long we might spend at each rung as we worked our way up the career ladder and what we would be paid at each new step along the way if we were truly crushing it.

He was laughing at me while writing it all on the board, but he could tell I was completely serious. Though starting salaries were around 66 percent of the top salaries for newly minted graduates, the retail salary numbers became quite large if you could move quickly up the organization, and I was burning into my brain the amount of time I would have to spend at each position and how much I might be earning in one, two, three, or more years after graduation. As it happened, four years later I was earning as much or more than my classmates who graduated with top starting salaries. I made a decision to go into department-store retailing. It was, after all, the field I had learned in my family's retail-furniture business and honed in college while working for a much larger retail-furniture operation in Austin. And it was hard work, which I knew could lead to competency and then respect if I was a good learner. While that was satisfying, I was also on a mission. But it was way bigger than just a career. I was trying to work up the nerve to ask Karleen Kaufman to marry me, and that was part of my plan.

How a Courtship Turns into a Strategic Plan

FOR MY CHRISTMAS BREAK DURING my second year at HBS, in December of 1975, I planned to spend the holiday with Bill Kaufman in San Antonio. We had been pledging brothers in the ZBT fraternity at UT and had remained close friends since. We had even taken a Caribbean cruise during the summer before I left for Boston. Bill was nothing if not fun to spend time with. He was a good-looking guy and attracted women everywhere he went. I liked just being in his general vicinity when he would go out—it increased the likelihood that I could spend time with a nice, good-looking woman. Since I had nothing to do and nowhere to go during that holiday break, I called Bill, and he said it would be great if I would come to visit. In college I had stayed with him in San Antonio several times, and I knew his parents and his younger sister Ann very well.

There was a third Kaufman sibling, who had never been in San Antonio when I was there—she was just a photo on a wall. But I definitely had noticed the photo on the wall! She had always been in some romantic locale like Russia or Africa while she was a student at Emory in Atlanta, Georgia, so I'd always missed meeting her during my time at UT. Now, in December of 1975, she was a second-year law student in San Antonio. On my first day visiting Bill, since he was working that day, he suggested that he would have his sisters come pick me up and take me to lunch. That was fine with me, and when Ann knocked on the door, I gave her a big hug.

We headed to her car, and when I got in, she introduced me to Karleen, who was sitting in the back seat. My heart literally skipped a beat and moved straight to my throat. I was mesmerized. For me, it was love at first sight. She was so beautiful I could barely take my eyes off of her in the rearview mirror, but I played it as cool as I could all the way to lunch. Lunch was a blur. She was playful, fun, and smart. I knew she was the person for me. I knew and loved her family already. I felt the Kaufman family was a lot like my family in that they were a small-town Jewish family. Her mother was cool and beautiful. And her father was an accomplished attorney and former city council member who spearheaded the move to desegregate San Antonio. I had always enjoyed spending time with Jack, respected his intellect, and loved that he was Karleen's father.

There was only one problem: Karleen was seriously dating one of my other ZBT fraternity brothers, and to make matters worse, he was also a student in her law school. For the next few days, we all went to movies and other activities together. Bill fixed me up with a lovely woman he knew in San Antonio, so I wasn't exactly a third wheel. But I determined that I would take on winning Karleen's heart as seriously as I did my other goals. I told myself that all my prior girlfriends had been dress rehearsals for my courtship of Karleen.

Since I was up to my eyeballs in case studies, it isn't surprising that I treated my courtship process like I would an HBS case study, in which strategy and marketing were the issues. I needed a solid marketing plan to attract Karleen, the same way companies had marketing plans to attract customers. Pretty soon my dorm room walls were filling with charts relating to timing for letters and phone calls, with conversation topics for each. There was a plan for how long between each letter or phone call. All I remember was that whatever I was doing was working. Karleen sure enough broke off with her other boyfriend early in the spring, reinforcing to me that the plan was working. I remember a more than $400 phone bill one month, which freaked me out. Though the phone bills were high, a call was where I learned that Karleen would want to live in San Francisco if she could live anywhere.

Our next opportunity to be together was my spring break. It was later in the spring, and by now I was completely serious about asking Karleen to marry me. I had to get a job to feel I had the best chance to get Karleen to say yes. I needed that icing for a proposal cake, so I headed to the HBS Placement Office to learn which companies based in the Bay Area were recruiting at school. I was trying hard to accommodate Karleen's location preference of San Francisco.

As it happened, two of the names were department stores headquartered in San Francisco. One was Macy's California, a division of Macy's New York, and the other was the Emporium, a division of Carter Hawley Hale Stores, which also owned Neiman Marcus in Dallas. Because I was taking the retailing class at HBS that semester and still had the May Company CEO's organization charts burned into my brain along with my furniture bona fides, I applied to both the Emporium and to Macy's. I was offered both jobs.

Macy's California was the hottest department store in America at that time, and its store in downtown San Francisco was second only to its flagship store in Manhattan in size and revenues. My bet was that no Harvard MBA had ever turned down a job offer from Macy's. Certainly two to three HBS graduates annually went to Macy's San Francisco. I had spent time with Phil Schlein, the charismatic Macy's CEO, and I thought he was spectacular. But I really liked Marvin Goldstein, a senior merchant at the Emporium, most. I felt I could learn more from Marvin and would get lots of exposure to the top management because they had never landed a Harvard MBA in San Francisco due to Macy's dominance in that market. Contrarian that I am, I figured I would have more of an unfettered path to the top at the Emporium than at Macy's, so I accepted the job at the Emporium.

With my job in hand, I went to San Antonio for spring break. I used the highly contrived champagne conceit (I was such a rookie, I thought it was a unique idea!) of dropping an engagement ring to the bottom of a champagne flute to start the conversation. I toasted Karleen, and when she indeed asked what was at the bottom of her champagne flute, completely encased in bubbles, I told her she had to drink all the champagne to the bottom of the glass in order to find out. When she pulled out the ring, I proposed to her properly and then said something to the effect of, "And, oh, by the way, I have a job in San Francisco." It worked! I was on my way back to Boston with a successfully conducted plan.

Shortly after the time I spent in San Antonio asking Karleen to marry me, we began our end of the MBA program activities at HBS. Because I was always living hand to mouth and couldn't afford to pay for Karleen's plane ticket to Boston, I worried I wouldn't be able to get her to Boston before I graduated, which would have been a travesty. Boston was so beautiful, especially in 1976, when it was the center of so many national activities around the bicentennial of the United States planned for that summer. I called the Texarkana National Bank, spoke with the president, who was friends with my father, and managed to borrow enough money to make it until I started my work in San Francisco. The purpose was really for me to continue courting Karleen, and feeling very flush with my new loan, I invited Karleen to see Boston. HBS was also in full bloom, and Karleen would get to meet all my classmates from my two years there. And as it happened, our section was planning a clambake on Cape Cod for the weekend Karleen would be with me, so Karleen had a world-class trip lined up.

The weekend was extraordinary, even though the start had me

ruffled. My buddies were all excited to meet Karleen, and when she arrived, they all came to my dorm room for introductions. Then they wouldn't leave! I tried every way I knew, but it became obvious this was their way of teasing us. They thought it would be great fun to not leave my room, even after all my prodding. When I finally succeeded in kicking them out, they went to the ground outside my window and started serenading us and throwing pebbles up to my fourth-floor dorm-room window. What a way to start our long weekend. But Cape Cod and the clambake compensated for the rough start.

My final exams were scheduled for the following Monday and Tuesday. Karleen waited outside in the beautiful May weather, while I dispensed with my finals as quickly as I could. Exams were like class-work: each exam was a new case study, and we had to read the case and outline it as if we were presenting it in class. My last scheduled exam was for marketing, a class where I had done an excellent job during the semester and had a very high average. The exam was the case of Ray-Ban sunglasses. I liked the professor a lot and felt it was mutual, so for my write-up, instead of making my case for the issues of Ray-Ban, I reminded the professor of all the ways I had done so well in his class that term. I then wrote that my fiancée was outside waiting for me to be finished with my exams, and I couldn't wait any longer to be with her. I asked him to please consider my body of work, but his exam was all that was keeping me away from Karleen, so I was going to turn in my blue book early so I could meet up with her. I was turning the final page on what had been a monumental achievement of a critical goal, and I felt very proud of myself. But my future was outside waiting, and I was so ready to go headlong into that bright future with Karleen in San Francisco. I indeed got an SAT—a satisfactory—for that course, which was good enough for me. I was graduating!

A storybook ending? Almost. When I got outside, Karleen told me we might have jumped the gun a bit on getting engaged because I had not first asked her parents if I could marry their daughter. I realized she was right, and I was mortified. But we were both sure that no one in San Antonio knew of our engagement, as we hadn't told anyone when I asked her to marry me. We decided I would take another trip to San Antonio so I could properly ask for Karleen's hand. With no time to stay in Boston for my graduation I drove directly to Texarkana and then on to San Antonio to take care of the one huge item I had screwed up. Her parents were so happy when I asked—it was like pushing on an open door—and we finally could start celebrating. I called my parents in Texarkana, and we told them also. The news was officially out.

Work on the wedding began quickly and furiously with an engagement party in Texarkana in early July before I left to start my new job at the end of July. Before I left San Antonio for San Francisco, Karleen's father, Jack, pulled me aside to give me an invaluable nugget of advice. He told me that there was getting married and there was being married. The getting-married part was full of lots of people's input and fraught with tension. The being-married part was for Karleen and me alone. I made sure during that autumn to steer clear of wedding planning and to focus on the prospect of being married. The lone exception was me letting the Kaufmans know that I hated dancing, was a really bad dancer, and didn't look forward to embarrassing myself by dancing.

Key Lessons

PART 2

Adapt to New Learning Environments:

Embrace different educational methodologies, like the
Socratic method, which may challenge traditional beliefs
and enhance critical thinking skills.

Recognize the Bearable Minimum:

Aim not always to be the best, but be good enough to
progress and succeed. Know your strengths and play
to them.

Master Pattern Recognition:

Look for patterns in data and experiences. This skill
can provide insights into complex problems and lead to
innovative solutions.

Counterintuitive Insights Are Valuable:

Sometimes the best solutions are not the most obvious
ones. Learning to think counterintuitively can open up new
paths to success.

Embrace Diverse Perspectives:

Encourage a variety of viewpoints in problem-solving
scenarios. Different backgrounds bring unique insights that
enrich the decision-making process.

Strategically Plan for Personal Goals:
Apply strategic thinking to personal ambitions, such as courtship or career moves. A well-thought-out plan can lead to fulfilling personal and professional relationships.

Negotiation and Persuasion Are Key:
Learn the art of negotiation and persuasion. These skills are crucial, whether securing a job or proposing marriage.

Value Mentorship and Leadership:
A great leader or mentor can inspire and teach important life and business lessons. Seek these relationships actively and learn from them.

Understand Your Financial Worth:
Recognize the value of your work, and don't be afraid to seek compensation that reflects your contribution.

Take Risks and Be Bold:
Sometimes the best opportunities come from taking the path less traveled. Be willing to take calculated risks.

Align Personal and Professional Goals:
Your career decisions should complement your personal life goals. Aligning them can lead to a more satisfying life.

Marriage Is a Partnership:
Understand that marriage is a partnership that extends beyond the wedding. It requires mutual respect, shared goals, and constant communication.

PART THREE

PARSING FOR PATTERNS

Thanks for Being One
of the Girls

I STARTED AT THE EMPORIUM in 1976, during the last week of July. On my first day of work, while they were trying to figure out where my first assignment should be, they sent me to the basement budget store to count the men's underwear for an inventory cycle count. I actually didn't mind it, but I felt that for $17,500 a year they would have been a bit more prepared for my first day. The dress code was a business suit. On that first day I sweated through my suit by noon. But Marvin Goldstein finally came around to greet me, so I began to think they actually knew I was there. I deemed it important that no matter the task, I would tackle it with a smile on my face, doing it perfectly and quickly.

By the end of the first week, I had been assigned to the junior sportswear division as a senior assistant buyer for junior tops. That meant our division bought all the clothes teenage girls might wear, and my particular buying office was in charge of buying all teen girls' tops. I reported to the buyer of junior tops.

I wish I could say that assignment was tough and there were some interpersonal issues I had to work through, but that would have been so much better than what actually happened. My first assignment was an unmitigated disaster for the first few months. Talk about pattern recognition: all through my time at HBS, I had read stories and even case studies about situations like what I was experiencing. We were taught that employees of companies that hired Harvard MBAs really hated the MBAs. They were paid more, jumped over everyone for promotions, and could be completely insufferable and cocky. One professor put it most succinctly—most employees would stay at work late to watch a Harvard MBA fail. I had been unaware that the junior division was the hottest, most fashion-forward, trendy part of the store, and people worked for years to get assigned to that division. It was where careers were made. And I was getting it from both ends. There were senior assistant buyers all over the store who had been vying for the open position I had been given. My boss had her own favorite, whom she had undoubtedly already told she would hire next. She was shocked to learn she had been given 1) a male and 2) an HBS grad. She was pissed off on both counts, and that is being polite. And everyone else at my level was pissed off also. They tried everything they could to run me off. There were petty things like telling me to go deliver something to the top floor when it was actually supposed to be delivered to the basement. It felt like the entire team was invested in my failure. And when they couldn't run me off with petty things, they pulled out their biggest cannon and aimed it straight at me, leading to the turning point in my relationship with the entire junior-division team in general and with Barbara in particular.

Around October 1, on a Friday afternoon (I will never forget the day of the week), I was taken into a very big room deep in the basement of the Emporium. It contained perhaps five hundred large totes of junior two-piece swimsuits. I was told it was the end-of-season remaining swimwear inventory that had been returned from all Emporium branch stores. These mismatched tops and bottoms had to be sorted with proper size bottoms matched with same size tops, tied together, marked down to a new lower price, and folded nicely to become the first swimwear sale the next spring. It looked like a job for a few people that could take days. I was told they would like it completely done by Monday morning. What they didn't know was that I was about as sick of their antics as they were of me. Since Karleen was in San Antonio, and I had nothing better to do, I decided to get myself locked in the store that night and work all through the weekend if necessary to get the job done. I did it, and I must say it was easier than getting the two carpet layers sober and finishing the job at Lake of the Pines. Come Monday morning, I took Barbara into the perfectly arranged storeroom with the five hundred totes out, labeled, and ordered—each with folded sets, priced right, and with a stack of markdown documents I had completed to show the value of the markdown. She was stunned silent, looking around, and she suddenly began laughing. She loved everything about it. I hadn't quit. I hadn't argued. I just did the serious grunge work without complaining, and she realized I had worked my rear end off all weekend to get the job done—neither of which she figured a Harvard MBA would do.

She congratulated me on a job well done and brought the entire division down to see my finished product. They were all pretty amazed, and I imagine they were secretly wondering if they could have pulled it off. From that day forward everything changed. Barbara and I got along famously, and the business did extraordinarily well. Everyone accepted me, and at Christmas I got a holiday card that said simply, "Thanks for being one of the girls," signed by each person in the entire junior division, not just my buying office. To this day, that remains my favorite card ever.

In January, six months after I had begun my job, I was promoted to buyer of budget women's pantsuits. I learned it was the fastest anyone had ever progressed to buyer level. And I got a raise, from $17,500 to $26,000 a year. I was definitely ahead of the aggressive timing and salaries that Dave Farrell had written on the board at HBS. The raise put me at a pay level with my classmates at HBS who had gone into the highest paying jobs in consulting, Wall Street, and Big Six accounting firms. I was quite proud of myself.

Putting a Ring on It

I HAD RENTED AN APARTMENT in the Pacific Heights area of San Francisco in July when I arrived so I could be close to the office and learn about the Bay Area before Karleen and I got married in January. My goal was to find a place where we could start our married life and get us all moved in so that when I brought Karleen to San Francisco after the San Antonio wedding we could walk into a new place, all furnished and ready for us. My parents had promised us furniture as our wedding present. They, of course, got the furniture-business discount, so it was great for them. And we couldn't afford furniture anyway, as I was still paying off my loan from the Texarkana National Bank. In addition, I had started to make payments on the HBS educational loan I had taken, as I hadn't had enough money saved to pay the $15,000 cost of two years at HBS. But now with my large (for me, compared to the $10,800 a year I was making at Holiday Bowl) starting salary and my raise when I became a buyer, I felt I could see my way to a day when I would have real money.

Karleen was finishing her law classes by December, and her plan was to come to San Francisco after the wedding, study to pass the Texas Bar Exam while I worked, and then pass the California Bar

Exam also in order to become a lawyer in San Francisco. She came to visit me once that autumn and truly loved the city. We drove over the Golden Gate Bridge and saw Sausalito and Tiburon. It was clear very quickly that was where we would be the happiest. Once she went back to San Antonio, I found a great townhouse with a beautiful view on the side of a hill in Tiburon and leased it. I had the new furniture moved in and the place settled by the time we arrived from San Antonio after our wedding.

Knowing that my only job for the wedding was showing up made me feel great. It had felt like I was woefully out of my depth even thinking about a wedding. I asked for an agenda of activities for the three days I would be in San Antonio, including Sunday, January 9, our actual wedding day. I packed everything I was told to bring, and off I went to my wedding and to start my new life with Karleen. The weekend was great! I had a bunch of my buddies from high school, college, and HBS all there. And even though he had turned down my request to be a groomsman, Julius drove down from Texarkana to attend. I remember standing under the chuppah and looking out at the mass of people at the wedding—and catching Julius's eye. When our eyes met, I had a moment—what a dear, sweet man, who had been so important to me in my life and had driven 450 miles to attend my wedding.

Our Stable Life
Gets Upended

KARLEEN WORKED HARD DURING THE six weeks after our wedding studying for the Texas Bar Exam and then flew back to Texas to take the exam. Because she wasn't in Texas to take the classes preparing students for the bar exam in person, she got access to a tape recorder and tape collection that played the classes she would have taken in person in San Antonio. She passed the Texas Bar Exam on her first try, and though Karleen had been sure when she arrived in California that passing the bar exams and going into California law practice was what she wanted to do, it took her just a little time watching me and learning what a job in retailing looked like to pivot into wanting a career in department-store retailing. I told her I felt it was really a shame that she was about to pivot after all the law school and after passing the Texas Bar Exam, but she was undeterred. As it would have been impossible for her to get a job at the Emporium, Macy's was the plum assignment. I called Phil Schlein, the CEO of Macy's California, who had been so good to me in the interview process and told him of Karleen's change of heart about law. He immediately set up interviews

71

for Karleen, and soon thereafter she began her job at Macy's California. Karleen was so happy and productive it seemed hard to believe she would have liked the law, so we both felt great about her new direction. We both were working very hard, from early until late every day.

But we really wanted to get out and enjoy the city. I knew that my cousin Sandy Furano lived in Sausalito, near Tiburon, with her husband Dave Furano. I called Sandy, and we all went to dinner and hit it off famously, becoming fast friends. Sandy was the life of every party. And she had managed to marry someone as vivacious as she was. Dave Furano had become the president of Bill Graham Presents, reporting to the legendary Bill Graham. Bill was hugely famous as America's first "rock impresario"—he was bringing the best rock artists from all over the United States and Europe to do tours in the United States. In the late 1960s he also had opened two of the biggest indoor venues for rock groups, Fillmore West in the Bay Area and Fillmore East in New York City, but he closed them in 1971 to focus on managing tours. Bill was and still remains a legend in the history of rock and roll.

Dave, Sandy, Karleen, and I started spending a lot of time together. Outside of work they were our social lifeline. We were definitely living vicariously through them. Dave was making ten times what I was making, literally, and their life was just outrageous. They spent the bulk of their time with huge rock stars. As president of Bill Graham Presents, Dave was the guy on the ground actually managing tours for groups ranging across the genre spectrum from the Rolling Stones, the Grateful Dead, and the Band to the other end of the spectrum with acts like John Denver and Barbra Streisand. Theirs was a life so exciting for us to follow. And I think perhaps we brought a bit of normalcy to theirs!

Then, chaos! One evening Dave started describing the future of rock concerts and talked in a very animated way about how that future absolutely belonged to the huge venues like outdoor sports stadiums. His point of view was informed by the outdoor concert series he and

Bill had started in the Oakland Coliseum called Days on the Green. It was an annual series of concerts that were meeting with enormous success. They were able to attract the biggest groups in the world because they could gather more than sixty thousand people for each concert. Dave told me that there was huge demand at each concert for any and all merchandise with the headline band's logos on it. The most wanted products were T-shirts, but there was also call for jackets, mugs, and other items so normal at sporting venues today but unheard of in the burgeoning outdoor rock concert business almost fifty years ago.

Dave was going to start a new business and call it Winterland Productions to develop and market products for the music industry with a focus on being the in-venue retailer for any concerts happening anywhere in America. He believed that this merchandising idea would become a huge business and thought I might be interested in becoming the CEO and developing the business. I was so honored to be asked, but my mind was swirling with how I could leave a very good gig at the Emporium, where I was already making $26,000, to take a flier on this new business. I was intrigued. Sandy and Dave said we should join them overnight for the next Days on the Green outdoor rock concert to see how an entire concert happens from start to finish. Dave felt that if I saw an outdoor concert from the ground up, I would know whether or not the business would be right for me. So, early in May 1977, Karleen and I met up with Dave and Sandy at the Oakland Coliseum to spend the night watching the stages get set and the artists prep for their performances. The headliners for this particular Days on the Green were Fleetwood Mac, the Doobie Brothers, Gary Wright, and, I believe, Dolly Parton. I wondered how in the world Dolly Parton fit with the other acts.

The high point of that long night of preparation came when Sandy and Dave told Karleen and me to join them at the crack of dawn on the top row of the Oakland Coliseum, looking to the east parking lots. Imagine standing on the top row of a stadium and gazing out toward huge chain-link fences cordoning off sections of the parking lots, the entire area shrouded with fog. There was a distinct din in the distance, but we couldn't see anything far away through the fog. Then, as minutes passed and the sun rose and began to cut through the fog, the largest speakers we had ever seen began pumping out the Beatles song "Here Comes the Sun" at the exact moment the sun burst through. In the distance huge gates swung open, and a roar hit us as tens of thousands of people burst through the gates, running full speed toward the entrance of the stadium below us. That scene still gives me chills just to write it. It is indelibly burned into my brain and will be for the rest of my life. I said yes to Dave.

When we got around to what I would be paid, he said $30,000 a year but there would be big bonuses and other perks. I told Dave I would take the job. Later that evening, Karleen suggested that I might want to call her father since he might have a different point of view to consider. She knew her father well, and I should have learned the lesson when I almost touched the third rail by not asking Karleen's parents' permission to marry their daughter before proposing to her. Jack Kaufman was a very conservative guy, as most men his age that I knew were in 1977, and he wasn't a fan of the hippie movement. He was also incredibly wise, as my Babbage's cofounder Jim McCurry and I later found out; he was our corporate attorney for our first five years. He was a person people sought out for advice, and he was always available for me. But he was also a product of his times, and this was a time when old-school white people felt very threatened by the hippie movement and anything that felt like counterculture. He was pretty sure that rock musicians fit that description.

Several things were at play: He was very clear that he didn't want his daughter to spend her life staying up all night with rock musicians at rock concerts. His daughter and her new husband were living in a city known for its Haight-Ashbury revolutionary culture. And I was only twenty-six years old and not very experienced in anything, having been raised in a small community in East Texas. I was also dutiful to a fault with elders by my midtwenties. I didn't want to start my marriage off on the wrong side of Karleen's parents. I already felt very close to them and loved the relationship they had with their children—so different from the relationships in my household! Additionally, I was a bit sympathetic to Jack's perspective, as the culture of Texarkana when I was growing up also revolved around people working for one company, building a long career, and earning a gold watch when they retired, just like in San Antonio.

Yes, the world was very different in 1977. I was naive, and San Francisco *was* the counterculture epicenter of the United States. Jack had been clear with his thoughts and feelings; I was dutiful and couldn't promise with 100 percent certainty that Winterland Productions would actually be successful. And I had seen nothing in my life to date that would prepare me for the nomadic life of following rock and roll tours around the world. I resolved that I had to back out of my commitment to move to Bill Graham Presents. Perhaps with this exception, Jack's advice to me both in business and in life was extraordinary. He was, as I called him for the rest of his life and when I describe him to my grandchildren, a wise old owl.

Thank goodness I had never mentioned any of this to anyone at the Emporium. It would have broken trust between me and the entire senior team who had bet on me when I was hired. Dave was very understanding but told me he had already told Bill I had accepted, so I needed to quickly find someone else to take the job. I did have an idea. A section mate of mine at HBS had gone to work at a Big Six accounting firm in San Francisco. His name was Don Hunt, and he had been a good friend. He had also played college football at the University of California at Davis and was a cool, smart, and athletic Bay Area guy. I took Don to lunch and told him he had to take the interview to help me save face, even if he didn't want the job. He interviewed and then quit his safe, high-paying job to take the helm as president of Winterland Productions, and over the next twenty years he made an enormous fortune. I have teased him since, saying I still haven't received my 3 percent finder's fee for setting him up. OK—only half teasing!

During the course of my career, I have built quite a lengthy list of missed business opportunities that add up to really large sums of money, and each is due to me taking a different fork in my road. Winterland Productions has the unique status of being the first on the list. Having said that, hindsight is twenty-twenty. What I can't and don't know is what twists and turns that gig took on in its development. I do know that you can't see around corners, and my bet is Don had surprises on his journey, as we all do.

On the positive side, the instability that had crept into our early marriage was alleviated. Almost as fast as I had started my first real job, I was presented with a job opportunity I had to think about. I was destabilized, worrying about what my reputation might become if I quickly quit a job I was quite lucky to land. I also worried about what would happen to our relationship with Sandy and Dave if I didn't take the job. I was definitely knocked off balance by the entire episode, and Karleen got her first look at what life with me might actually be like. I think we were both relieved when our lives returned to what they had been before this chaotic episode. This was the time in my life when I was collecting a great many completely new experiences, and this episode was one of those on so many levels.

Sandy and Dave had dinner with us soon after Don took the job as CEO of Winterland Productions and assured us they weren't pissed. They also told us that since they hadn't gotten us a wedding present yet, they would like to give us two airline tickets to Hawaii as our belated wedding gift.

Napoleon Was Correct!

THAT SPRING FOLLOWING OUR WEDDING, we became more and more friendly with Marvin. He was a Jewish single guy, so we started having him over for dinner and vice versa. I had to be careful at work not to mention his name or anything about our budding relationship. Corporate politics is tricky in normal situations, but it can become a blood sport in unusual circumstances. I had already survived my first brush with corporate politics, which ended when I organized the swimwear. There was no doubt in my mind that if word got out that I was friends with Marvin Goldstein, my boss's boss, I would be right back in the crosshairs of the corporate gossip. I had already been given enough of the grief I had been told to expect as a Harvard MBA, and I wasn't interested in poking that corporate bear again if I could help it. More importantly, I knew I had to prove every day that I was a solid merchant worthy of the fast track I was on. Winning one assignment was not enough. I needed to continue putting points on the board if I wanted to remain on the fast track.

It didn't hurt that I was crushing my new buying assignment. There is an old adage attributed to Napoleon: "If you want to know what is happening on the front lines, go look." I buy into that 100

percent, and I have my entire career. The inventory I was responsible for
was displayed on the main floor of the downtown flagship Emporium
store. It was now the early summer of 1977. I was twenty-six years old.
I spent a significant amount of my time on the floor meeting customers,
helping customers, and making sure we were keeping them satisfied.
I did notice that though it was summer, it was very cold in downtown
San Francisco, which I learned was just the regular weather pattern
in Northern California. The major cable car turnaround for the entire
San Francisco cable car system was right in front of our downtown
flagship store. The cable car turnaround was where all the tourists
jumped onto and off of the cable cars, and every day there was a steady
stream of tourists coming into the Emporium in their white shorts and
knit T-shirts, looking for sweaters and coats. If you weren't from San
Francisco, the summer cold was a very big surprise.

In spite of that weather knowledge, the flagship Emporium had
no cold-weather apparel on the floor in the summer, though we should
have. We did have a huge amount of winter sweaters and jackets off
the floor, waiting for the next fall season. I went and began moving
boxes from storage to the selling floor. I promptly got in trouble with
the Retail Workers Union for doing a union job, but I ultimately got
the floor full of the warmer clothes the tourists wanted. The business
exploded! I was putting a large number of points on the board, and
it wasn't lost on anyone. Pretty soon Marvin was bringing divisional
managers from other merchandise areas down to our floor location to
explain what I had done and the result.

Finding Gold in Sacramento

ONE THING I LEARNED WORKING in a big corporation was that there was a steady drumbeat of "Employee Communications" press releases informing everyone about who was leaving the company, who was being promoted, or who from the outside was being brought into the company to fill a vacant position.

The Emporium was no exception, but in the fall of 1978, I was surprised to read a release saying Marvin Goldstein was going to move to Sacramento to head up all merchandising at Weinstock's, another division of Carter Hawley Hale stores. I was completely surprised Marvin hadn't told me before the communications release, and Karleen and I were going to be very sad to lose our relationship with Marvin. Or so we thought. The next day I received a call from Marvin inviting me to move to Sacramento with him to become division merchandise manager over all junior sportswear, women's dresses, coats, furs, and maternity. I was pretty blown away by the offer. I was virtually certain that no one in any major department store had made it from training squad to DMM in slightly more than two years and at more than triple the salary of the one they had started with. I had blown past Dave Farrell's org chart for sure! When Karleen told Macy's about our impending move, they immediately offered her a job at their Sacramento store. Since she was very pregnant with Ben, Karleen and Macy's agreed that she would be on maternity leave until after Ben was born.

Life is what happens while you're planning for your future! Climbing the corporate ladder and finding ourselves in Sacramento was a great example of that truth. Our life began getting real and happening right under our noses. It's impossible to divorce your work life from your family life, and each impacts the other. You can't appreciate that until you live it, and this was our first experience of that. Additionally, somewhere in there is supposed to be work-life balance, though for the biggest part of our early marriage and work years it didn't feel like there was any balance. Frankly, that didn't bother us because we felt we were investing in our future, and that meant, in this case, a detour to a city we were not excited about and to a division of the company that I knew little about. Moving for a promotion within a company was a pretty standard business practice back then, and one that Karleen and I embraced. Our goal was to eventually work our way back to Texas, and we knew this promotion could be important to achieving that goal in the long term. We both knew I had to continue doing well in each successive position, so it did feel to us like our move to Sacramento, symbolically at least, proved our career was progressing very nicely. Plus, I was continuing to gain experiences, each of which impacted me and helped me think about how a highly functioning company should operate and hone my management style as I continued to climb the corporate ladder.

My work in the junior department at the Emporium really did give me a great foundation for my work at Weinstock's. The Emporium had buyers with great taste levels, and we had all sorts of reports and processes to understand elements like which trends were emerging and which were in decline. I was able to bring that process approach to Weinstock's—along with help and direction from Marvin. I knew that to keep my upward career trajectory I had to do something very special to drive our business higher than anyone thought I could. And I was now reporting directly to Marvin, who reported directly to the CEO, so my visibility within Weinstock's was quite high. It would be huge if I could find a trend in junior apparel that hadn't been discovered yet by our competitors, have great success with that trend, and give Weinstock's great fashion credibility. That was what the retail game was all about. Establishing your store as the headquarters for the newest and hottest fashions was the goal of all fashion retailers, and my junior division could be the division that led the way.

A couple of years later, when I was in a different city in a different company and with a next-level job at the ripe old age of twenty-eight, I was asked in an interview how it could be that I was promoted from a DMM role at a small division of a large company with presence only in Sacramento, Reno, and Utah, to a VP-GMM position, a much bigger title and job, at one of the top department-store groups in America, with dominance in North Texas, Oklahoma, and Arizona. It was a little like skipping college football and going directly to the pros. It was unheard of in every way. I had moved from the training squad to VP and general merchandise manager in less than four years. By comparison, Dave Farrell's organization chart suggested that it would take twelve years to get from the training squad to GMM!

It wasn't my brains or anything like that. I reported that it was our babysitter in Sacramento who changed our lives. When I was in the junior sportswear division at the Emporium, I learned that you had to go see your teen customers "in the wild" to understand what apparel they were actually wearing and then to ensure that you brought the right products into the assortments to satisfy them. The junior division was always the trendiest division in the store, and the only way for a store to stay on top of trends was to go where the young people hung out and just watch. If you were in the junior business, it was part of your job description. It became part of what I did, no matter where I was: check to see what the teen girls were wearing, and ensure those fashions were very well represented in our assortments.

Our neighborhood in Fair Oaks, California, was full of young families, and we found a young teen living down the street who was looking for a steady babysitting gig. Karleen and I were looking for date nights on a regular basis, so it was easy to lock down our sitter for every Saturday night. I was always conscious of what she was wearing, as it was essential to our junior sportswear at Weinstock's that we win the fashion wars in our community.

One night in early 1980 she walked into our house to babysit wearing a pair of Dickies painter's pants, with the little cloth painter hooks around the waist. True painter's pant design. It was a nice white pair of pants and looked like something we should have at Weinstock's but didn't. So I peppered her with questions. It turned out that she purchased the painter's pants in a work-clothing store and that it was the hottest thing among her friends and almost impossible to find.

That following Monday morning, I called Britannia Jeans and asked them about painter's pants. They volunteered that they were working as fast as they could but couldn't keep up with the demand from their small specialty-store accounts. After several other calls, I was convinced that this was the next big thing. I walked into Marvin's office and told him what I'd learned and he agreed we should make a large buying commitment and create a huge display in the downtown Weinstock's flagship store. We assembled the heads of display and advertising and developed a plan while our orders were being sewn and sent to our floors. We took a large, high-traffic corner of our downtown flagship's floor and constructed a billboard with scaffolding in front of it. We had junior-sized female mannequins all dressed in painter jeans and painter hats up and down the scaffolding and across the billboard. We announced ourselves as the headquarters for painter's pants. Because we had caught this trend so early relative to our large department-store counterparts, I had placed huge orders with all the important denim suppliers, all of whom were trying to catch the emerging demand. They were very supportive of Weinstock's, as we indeed were first in the nation among large department stores to catch the trend. It was working remarkably well. Marvin and I would walk down to the first floor and watch people interact with the impressive display and then walk to the racks and buy a pair or two of painter's pants. We also noted that lots of Macy's officials were walking in to see our display, and some were even boldly taking photos.

One day I got a call from the switchboard, and they told me a person had asked for me, requesting that I meet him on the main floor: not by name but rather "the junior sportswear DMM." I was curious and walked down to the floor and met Chuck Griffin, the EVP of merchandising of Sanger-Harris stores in Dallas. Sanger-Harris was a division of Federated Department Stores (FDS), the largest confederation of department stores in America. FDS owned all the biggest and best department-store nameplates in America, which included Bloomingdale's, Filene's, Burdines, Rich's, Foley's, and Bullock's, among many others. He asked me a ton of questions about how I came up with the trend. But he also asked me questions about myself and my history in retailing. I could tell he was interviewing me. He told me he would head back to Dallas and then we could find a later time when I might fly to Dallas to meet him there. We shook hands, and that was that. Except, as I told Karleen later that night, though my goal at Carter Hawley Hale stores was to ultimately get transferred to their Neiman Marcus division in Dallas, I would also be plenty happy to head home to Texas if the job was with Federated Department Stores at their Sanger-Harris division. And Karleen was ready also—with a new child, she wanted to be closer to family in Texas. Even though Macy's kept calling and asking when she wanted to come back to work, she was loving hanging out with Ben every day. It ended up that until our fourth child left home for college, Karleen never went back to a formal job—she was just too darn good at raising four spectacular children!

The stars aligned during my visit to Dallas. I learned that the chairman of Sanger-Harris, Don Stone, had just been promoted to president of Federated Department Stores and would be moving to Cincinnati, where Federated Department Stores was headquartered. The president of Sanger-Harris, Jack Miller, was going to become chairman and CEO at Sanger-Harris. Chuck Griffin, whom I had met in Sacramento, was going to become the new president of Sanger-Harris. They were actually looking for a new general merchandise manager to be in charge of children's, cosmetics, accessories, and fine jewelry. When Don Stone interviewed me, we both discovered that he had not only gone to UT, as I had, but also that he and my father-in-law, Jack Kaufman, had been fraternity brothers and college roommates. Couple that with the fact that Sanger-Harris was well known in the world of department stores as one of the fastest growing, most highly profitable divisions of FDS, and it seemed like the perfect time to end our journey through California to come back home to Texas. Dallas was geographically smack in between Texarkana and San Antonio, so we would be close to both of our families. And we could begin to grow our own family, as it was clear by that time that we both wanted more kids.

My First Lessons in Firing People

JUST AS IT IS CRITICAL to hire the right people for the right positions, it is equally critical to know when you have tried all you can to help someone be successful but finally realize they simply don't have the skills to succeed. I have two stories about firing people courtesy of Weinstock's and Marvin, one with a happy ending and one with a lifetime lesson. The third lesson came from Jack Welch, the storied CEO of General Electric, much later in my career, but equally formative.

When I took the divisional merchandising manager job at Weinstock's, all the positions were filled. Marvin told me that it was my decision but he felt I would want to fire Virginia Williams, the buyer of maternity, bridal, coats, and furs. To say Virginia was an old-school retail buyer would be a gross understatement. She refused to use modern sell-through reports, instead using an old notebook where she soldiered sales of each item at each store on a grid. Virginia had already been relegated to the buying area of the store—certifiably dead-end work. I'm guessing she was in her early seventies, and I was a whopping twenty-seven years old. She and I sat down for our first meeting, and she was remarkably candid. She told me that everyone had been out to fire her for years, but no one could get around to it. And that, she said, was because her results were great. All year, every year, in the toughest departments in the store, she excelled. I acknowledged that I had been told I would probably want to fire her, and I had said I would hold off until I got to know her better. She asked me if I would please go into the market with her for half a day on our division's next New York buying trip. I was fine with that. Long story short, Virginia was a spectacular one-woman wrecking machine of a buyer. She would take wedding dresses not sewn to agreed-upon specifications back into bridal showrooms and sling the box across the floor at the vendor representative. She was just tough as nails in all ways, and she was also very successful. She didn't need modern reports; she was able to get the results she needed by calling stores and doing things her way. It didn't hurt that her buying duties were very contained, and individual store managers in charge of her areas were happy to call her a couple of times a week to give her sell-through information. I felt she was making a contribution and wasn't a candidate for firing. Virginia and I became fast friends and were the original odd couple. Her business continued improving, her attitude improved, but she never, as far as I know, changed her method of gathering information and working in the market. She remained with the company for the duration of my tour of duty there. I only wish I knew what happened to her after I left.

I fired my first person while at Weinstock's, a dress buyer with a long record of bad results. Marvin was new at Weinstock's also, and he had resolved to clean house of all the underperformers. She happened to be on his list. Did I learn a lesson! I fired her on December 15, without really thinking about the calendar. She yelled at me when I fired her, not for firing her, but for doing it on December 15, in the middle of the holiday season. To add insult to injury, she actually reached for a blackboard eraser behind her, threw it at me, and stormed out of the room. I was fairly mortified. I have reflected on this more than once in my career since and decided that if you are going to fire someone, you can't do it after November 15 or before January 15. That is my blackout window. You should never fire anyone right after Christmas because that is when the person's expenses are highest from all the holiday gift costs. And you shouldn't fire anyone just before the holidays, as it doubles the impact of the blow to them. I decided on a sixty-day termination moratorium annually, and I pretty much stuck to that the rest of my career.

I do have to come clean about firing the dress buyer because I learned one of the top lessons of my business career during this exercise, courtesy of Marvin. The fact is that I had agreed to fire the dress buyer at least six weeks before I actually did fire her, shortly after starting my work at Weinstock's. And each week Marvin would ask me whether I had fired her yet, and I would say no, always giving some new reason. Finally, in one weekly meeting, Marvin said something like this: "I know you're nervous about firing her, and I remember when I fired my first person. It is tough. I will tell you what. I'm happy to do this for you. Let me fire her. I have fired so many people, and it won't be an issue for me." I said no, that I would do it. When he offered again and said it would really be no problem, I said OK. If it wasn't a problem, he should go ahead and fire her. He said, "Great, no problem," and then swung around in his desk chair, picked up the phone, and dialed the head of HR. He told the HR person to send my next paycheck directly to him instead of to me. I'm guessing the blood had drained from my face when he hung up because he swung back around in his chair and asked what was the matter. I told him I needed that paycheck. He then told me that we do the work we love in retailing for free but that we earn our paychecks for doing things we don't want to do. If I didn't want to fire the dress buyer, he would be happy to, but he wanted my paycheck. Lesson learned. I have used that conversation more than once in my career to coach more junior people who reported to me. It was amazing how many people you could catch in the "no problem, I'll handle it for you" web!

It's important to note that had I just fired her when Marvin and I had the original conversation around November 1, I wouldn't have learned the horrible yet important lesson about the timing of firing people. I no doubt would have learned it later, but not during my first employee termination.

As I was working in the corporate world, I started realizing that while pattern recognition can come prepackaged in an educational environment like HBS, the best learnings about pattern recognition come in the heat of battle in the corporate world.

Key Lessons

PART 3

Embrace Versatility in Your Role:

Be open to diverse responsibilities and learn from each one.
From operations to customer service, each facet adds to
a holistic understanding of business.

Recognize and Adapt to Market Demands:

Stay attuned to customer preferences, and be ready to adjust
your inventory and strategy accordingly, as illustrated by the
painter's pants trend.

Value Mentorship:

Engage with mentors like Marvin, who can provide
guidance, push your limits, and help navigate corporate
politics and personal development.

Persistence Pays Off:

In negotiations and business dealings, persistence can be as
crucial as acumen. Stick to your guns when you believe in
the outcome.

Handle Termination with Care:

Firing is a necessary but difficult part of management.
Do it with consideration for timing and the individual's
circumstances.

Balance Work and Family Life:
Professional decisions impact family life and vice versa.
Strive for a balance that respects both spheres.

Geography Matters:
Consider location and commute in job decisions. Quality of
life can be as important as the job itself.

Build a Solid Reputation:
Consistently delivering results and proving yourself in
various roles builds a reputation that can fast-track career
advancement.

Be Adaptable in Personal and Professional Life:
Be ready to shift gears, whether it's moving to a new city for
a job opportunity or changing career paths.

Networking and Relationships Matter:
Maintain connections and relationships; you never know
how a familial or collegiate connection might influence your
career path.

Family as a Cornerstone:
The birth of a child is a pivotal moment that reshapes
priorities and perspectives, intertwining deeply with career
choices and life decisions.

PART FOUR

PATTERN RECOGNITION COMES ALIVE

Data Is Oxygen

I WAS TWENTY-EIGHT, ALMOST TWENTY-NINE, when I started working at Sanger-Harris. I spent two and a half years there and honed my skills in the world of fashion retailing. This was mostly due to the fact that the children's division at Sanger-Harris had the greatest group of trendy young buyers in the store. They were so much fun to be around, but they were completely focused and incredibly aggressive when it came to ordering and financial planning. And they all got along famously! Their boss, Ed Ebinger, reported to me. In this part of the retail business, it is all about how much inventory you can put on the floor, how much floor space you can get dedicated to your product, and what gross margin you can generate with that inventory and floor space. Ed owned responsibility for all those issues and reported to me.

It was pretty clear that the buyers always got what they wanted from Ed in terms of inventory and floor space. Ed was mostly along for the ride, not giving them much direction at all and just enjoying their results. And while their results were fabulous, their inventories were growing faster than their sales. The children's division floor space was encroaching on other business's floor space. There is a fine line to walk when you're in charge of all merchandise in a store division. Ed was in charge of filling his allocated floor space but was letting his floor space and merchandise creep pretty incessantly into that of other divisions. His numbers were so good that few people argued. And even though I understood why Ed essentially was just getting out of his buyers' way, I knew I wasn't going to be able to move the needle with my results by just riding their coattails.

I was determined to make them work for their extra inventory purchases above the financial plan and sales projections they had already agreed to. I taught them gross margin return on investment (GMROI), which was new to them. Essentially, to be successful with GMROI, you had to sell your inventory faster and with fewer markdowns. That becomes much trickier than just buying more and more merchandise and requires discipline in making hard decisions about what to buy and what not to buy, along with how much to order up front and then how much with reorders. This group of buyers continually rose to the occasion and continued to leave me hugely impressed and mostly proud of them. I way overindexed on time spent in the market in the children's division because of the impact of their division on both my and Sanger-Harris's total results. And I believed they could continue making even greater progress with the children's department results, which they did.

Each division of Federated Department Stores was part of the same buying group called Affiliated Merchandise Corporation (AMC). This group made special purchases that it would offer to members who wanted unique merchandise to present to their customers. In addition, the AMC group collected information from its members regarding sales and gross margin results for each separate merchandising group within each member of FDS. So I could compare my Sanger-Harris children's division same-store sales results and actual gross margin results against every other children's division reporting results to AMC. The book, published monthly and called *The Red Book*, was available to each member.

I am a data-driven operator. When I saw a sister division of Federated Department Stores delivering better results in any of my areas, I would pick up the phone and call my counterpart to discuss their business and perhaps find ways I could improve. *The Red Book* was a terrific tool, and I used it regularly. I believe in numbers, and until I can dive deeply into numbers to understand subtleties and nuances, I don't tend to take anyone's words as truth in business.

The Red Book was a treasure trove of learning for me, not just about department-store retailing but also about retailing in general. It was easy to see that, for instance, the Limited was growing its national business much faster than FDS. So was the Children's Place, a specialty store selling all children's items. So as proud as I was about our children's business, I had to be sober enough to acknowledge that the Children's Place was growing faster than any single division of FDS and faster than FDS's total children's business. I believed that to be true of virtually all specialty retail concepts. For instance, Zales jewelry was growing the fine jewelry business faster than any single division of FDS and even faster than all of FDS. And Zales was expanding coast-to-coast and winning the retail-jewelry wars against FDS. These are just examples, but I'm not sure if I would have been able to find any national specialty-store chain that was *not* growing faster than FDS.

I expected that the top officers of FDS were examining this information also, and since the best and brightest merchants in department stores tended to work at FDS, I consistently compared myself to them. I was sure they were doing the same with me. For one quarter about a year into my tenure at Sanger-Harris, each of my four divisions was number one in its sector of *The Red Book*. While all that was good, and I figured my performance was being followed at headquarters, I was most focused on the state of retailing in general, how we were getting beaten in any category in which a strong specialty retailer was emerging. Retailing in general was undergoing a massive change. A pattern was emerging, and it didn't bode well for department stores.

The Changing Retail Landscape

IN THE 1960s, 1970s, and 1980s, major regional enclosed malls were being built all over America, anchored by department stores like Sanger-Harris. But something insidious was also happening under the rooftops of these emerging malls, and I suspected that department-store executives were too busy with their rapid expansions to worry about where the next big competitor or disruptor would come from. In addition to rapid growth opportunities for the anchor tenant department stores, specialty-store chains were emerging rapidly to fill the open spaces inside the cavernous malls that needed many new and smaller tenants. As a result, the most popular specialty stores were growing much, much faster than even the fastest-growing department stores. These specialty-store concepts were developing their own merchandise designs and getting that merchandise made in China. Most ominously, these new specialty chains tended to be stores specializing in the highest-growth and highest-margin departments inside of department stores.

Think about the specialty stores that were exploding in size, location, revenues, and profits at the same time I was viewing the FDS data. They had names they used all across America for greater national name recognition than department stores, which had disparate names in different geographies: the Emporium in the Bay Area; Weinstock's in Sacramento, California's San Joaquin Valley, Nevada, and Utah; and Sanger-Harris in Texas, Oklahoma, and Arizona. Explosive-growth specialty stores included names like the Gap, which sold high-margin denim jeans; the Limited, which sold women's fashion apparel; a start-up called Victoria's Secret, which sold intimate apparel; Zales jewelry; the Children's Place; and others. I could go on and on, but it was becoming obvious to me that these specialty-store chains represented an existential threat for department stores. They could move faster than department stores, operating under one name brand from coast-to-coast versus the highly fragmented nameplates of the major department stores. Those factors gave these specialty stores serious advantages over department stores, with scale in advertising, operations management, technology, and virtually every functional area of retailing. As I toured each Sanger-Harris store on a regular basis, I also walked each mall where we were an anchor. I was repeatedly blown away by the number of big-name specialty stores popping up in every mall where we operated. I got knots in my stomach viewing their assortments, the wonderful merchandising of their products, and the sheer number of customers who were shopping in their stores. It was very shocking to me that department stores appeared to be whistling past their own graveyards. I felt I had to shine a light on this emerging risk, not just at Sanger-Harris, but across FDS. The data was not only available from *The Red Book*, but also from simply reading the business press. And, most importantly, it was apparent from walking the emerging regional enclosed malls, all of which had growing national specialty-store chains that were taking increasing market share from the department stores.

Inside Sanger-Harris, I began pitching the president and chairman the idea that if FDS wanted to respond to the emergence of specialty stores, the best way to start might be to begin combining divisions of its network. I was suggesting perhaps combining Foley's in Houston with Sanger-Harris in Dallas—I was agnostic about which nameplate to keep and which one to bury. I was sure the synergies of the two largest markets in Texas could be huge, but I really touched the third rail expressing that thought. It appeared to be heresy within FDS to even have a conversation about combining divisions. Nevertheless, I was sure I was correct and continued making my case by analyzing the biggest, fastest emerging specialty brands and presenting the analysis to my boss. I was able to link each concept without exception to one of our highest-gross-margin areas of the store, and I further proved with data that specialty-store growth was eroding our margins. Essentially, specialty stores were exploding at the expense of department stores. I will never forget the presentation I made to Chuck Griffin, my boss, in early 1982. My hypothesis was this: when any category of consumer goods reaches measurable size (for 1981 I called measurable size $1 billion minimum in revenues) the specialty-store channel would become an important, if not dominant, channel of distribution in that category. It was so easy to point to the Limited, with its stores named Limited, Limited Express, Victoria's Secret, and more. Jewelry chains like Zales were growing dramatically. Foot Locker was owning the mall shoe business. I could go on and on. I worked on that presentation very hard, and when I presented it to Chuck, after a bunch of questions, he got up, walked around his office, scratched his chin, and said (and I will never forget the exact words), "I will not be intimidated by the facts." Think about that for a minute. Case closed.

Another instance later that year also underscored that my hypothesis was correct. The cosmetics division at Sanger-Harris also reported to me and was managed by Linda Knight, who was a force of nature in that division. You never wanted to stand between Linda and whatever was her passion of the moment. If you did, you would get steamrolled. In the face of Neiman Marcus's huge presence with all the Estée Lauder brands, including Clinique, at the Dallas NorthPark Neiman Marcus store, and the NorthPark Neiman's having the largest Clinique business in America outside of New York City, Linda nevertheless convinced Leonard Lauder to allow Sanger-Harris to launch its first Clinique counter outside of Neiman Marcus in Dallas at the Sanger-Harris store in the Preston Center, less than three short miles from NorthPark.

This was a huge deal—Neiman Marcus believed they had an exclusive in Dallas for all Estée Lauder and Clinique businesses. We even heard that Stanley Marcus himself had gone to New York City to argue with Leonard Lauder about the decision. But it was quite a good decision for Estée Lauder. In its first year open at the Sanger-Harris Preston Center location, Clinique generated $2.8 million in cosmetics revenue, making it the largest first-year Clinique revenue ever in any single location. We assumed we had knocked off the Estée Lauder blinders in favor of Neiman Marcus and that we could expect another two to four Clinique locations to open in other Sanger-Harris locations during the next year or two. Leonard Lauder planned a trip to Dallas to see the Preston Center store. I had all the data ready to make the argument to expand further with Sanger-Harris. Our CEO, Jack Miller, and president, Chuck Griffin, both attended the meeting. It was a big deal, and we had high expectations. Leonard surprised us early in the meeting by saying something to the effect of, "We are managing Estée Lauder for the year 2000, and as such, we have no plans to open any additional doors at Sanger-Harris for the foreseeable future." We were all stunned, but they *were* managing their business for the year 2000 and clearly felt new trends were emerging that would impact their sector. They were opting to wait to learn more about the next generation of retailing in general and cosmetics specifically before reacting.

Seeds of Leadership Principles

I WAS VERY YOUNG WHEN I joined Sanger-Harris, twenty-eight years old, and I had been promoted so quickly. I had very little actual corporate experience other than the seven hundred case studies at HBS. I had definitely honed my pattern recognition at Harvard, but the reality was that I had been born and raised in a small town with no large corporations. Essentially, since graduation from HBS, I had awakened to a new business world each day. I had already seen so much in such rapid succession in my career that it was almost destabilizing for me. Completely alien experiences included:

- Being the target of corporate-culture backlash at the Emporium in the junior sportswear division and surviving and thriving. I could see it coming from a mile away due to my HBS learnings, but until you experience something like that for yourself, the studying is simply academic.
- Being exposed to the countercultural center of the hippie movement in San Francisco and being given the opportunity

to join the rock and roll epicenter of that movement.
If I had an HBS case study written about me at that time
in my career, the Winterland Productions case would have
been profound!

- Experiencing the payoff for being the first merchant to
  identify and exploit a major new fashion trend—juniors
  painter's pants—resulting in a job offer way beyond my
  experience level. I had caught lightning in a bottle and
  certainly made the most of it, but there is no question it was
  the first time I was in the limelight for my work at this level.

- Being pushed by a billionaire, Ross Perot, to leave the corporate world and be funded to start my own entrepreneurial
  venture. (More on this soon!) So many lessons there, not
  the least of which, for me, was that no matter the wealth,
  everyone puts their pants on one leg at a time!

There were other experiences, but the big point, I realized, was that
I had not had time to digest what I was learning and experiencing.
How was I supposed to feel about the world of large corporate work?
Was I supposed to not ask questions and just exploit my opportunities
for maximum payback? Just get along by going along with the business
practices in place? These were very big issues for me, and while it didn't
seem like I should just keep moving with the flow, I hadn't had time
to process the lightning-fast progression over what had only been four
short years.

Two other stories from this Sanger-Harris period illustrate additional experiences that finally led me to formally begin thinking about
the value of formulating a set of principles in my head that could guide
my own decision-making when facing future strategic business issues.
I already had developed a set of rules to guide decision-making at the
tactical level—they took the pressure off when you found yourself at
some critical juncture with pressure to respond or perform. If you had
a set of preset rules to guide decision-making, it could take the heat off

any tough situation in real time. For example, if the GMROI wasn't at a certain level, we would absolutely rethink floor space and buying practices. If I had to make those decisions one at a time as issues surfaced, I would spend too much time retracing old steps. But decision rules are for dictating actions at a tactical level—the specific daily work that is done.

I was beginning to think about decision rules to dictate actions at a strategic level. They would shine a bright light on strategic issues and be universal enough to apply to big issues like intellectual honesty or integrity. For instance, how was I supposed to react to being told by my boss that he wouldn't be intimidated by the facts? Was that OK, or was it intellectually sloppy? I thought I knew, but I couldn't be sure, as I hadn't heard those words before from a boss.

Other similar questions and concerns emerged during my Sanger-Harris years that prompted me to think about developing some Leadership Principles. The answers weren't obvious to me at the time and certainly took another ten years of experiences to begin to crystalize. Just as I had kept my own counsel as a child, I didn't talk about what I was thinking to anyone because I didn't have answers. I was looking for a construct to help formalize how I could consistently think about tough issues. I had plenty of quiet time to reflect on my career and what I was experiencing during flights as I traveled to meet suppliers. Airplanes became my respite from the fast-paced business world where I was working. The Estée Lauder story was an example. Was it OK for Estée Lauder to not care about the needs of Sanger-Harris by refusing to allow us to put their products in other stores in our network? What did I think about a company that managed its business for a point twenty years in the future? How could I be mad at them? What is the smart-business reaction to learning that kernel of information from the CEO of such an enormous and critically important supplier? Those were the things I could think about when staring out the window of an airplane.

The two other stories that incited my desire for leadership principles were both about people and what happens when conflicts emerge
between corporate strategy and the lives of the people who are in
charge of executing the strategy.

Ed Ebinger was our DMM of the children's division. As I mentioned earlier, there was no question that the children's buyers played
Ed like a fiddle on everything having to do with financial planning,
floor layouts, turnover requirements, and more. His buyers as a group
were the smartest and most competent buying group I had in my areas
of responsibility. But Ed wasn't doing anything to push them smarter,
harder, better, or faster, which is, after all, the job of a supervisor. My
point of view was that because we had so many other burning issues,
the priority of making a move on Ed was very low. However, it was
the opinion of Jack Miller and Chuck Griffin, who had worked with
him for years before I arrived, that we needed a stronger children's
DMM and that I should fire Ed. I had no problem with that and did
as I was told.

My feelings at the time were a far cry from my reticence to fire an
employee at Weinstock's a short two years earlier. It took almost no
time for him to file a lawsuit against Sanger-Harris for age discrimination. When our lawyers came back, their math suggested that since
I was twenty-eight years old, about half Ed's age, and all the buyers
were young also, that Federated Department Stores would likely lose
a jury trial and have to pay Ed more than $1 million to settle his age
discrimination lawsuit.

In retrospect, Ed's firing was the definition of age discrimination, although I didn't see that when I followed orders and fired him.
I was hired as a twenty-eight-year-old into a position way beyond my
experience level and, frankly, perhaps my capabilities. Ed was in his
midfifties and had overseen an area that for many years was arguably
the best-performing merchandising division in Sanger-Harris. Ed
could have argued in court that Sanger-Harris wanted youth at all

costs and he was performing very well and could illustrate it with his results. And I was a young, unproven executive who arguably also just wanted more youth in Ed's position, so he was fired for no good reason, just for being too old. It didn't matter that I had no problem with Ed's age or that I was simply following orders by firing him. The surrounding events told a different story—and the company was exposed to big trouble because of it.

All of a sudden, people at FDS and Sanger-Harris got cold feet, and I was told I had to rehire Ed and let him continue with his job. Imagine how awkward that was for both Ed and me. I was shocked that an outcome that would likely have been predictable to senior executives could have happened without anyone in charge bothering to even get a lawyer's input at the outset. You can imagine how much fodder that was for my long airplane flights!

The second story had to do with FDS CEO Howard Goldfeder's annual all-day meeting with the Sanger-Harris senior team. In that annual meeting, Howard would review the last twelve months' actual results at Sanger-Harris as well as our plans for the next twelve months. Howard was known as a very gruff guy who chewed people up in meetings attended by large groups of people. I went overboard in preparing for my part of the agenda. At this time all shoe departments at Sanger-Harris were leased by a St. Louis company that paid us 10 percent of their revenues for the right to manage all the shoe departments.

The question to be resolved with Mr. Goldfeder in the room was whether or not we should be allowed to take back our women's shoe department and run it ourselves. My argument, supported by facts, was that we should take it back. At the end of the discussion with me, Howard said, "Are you willing to bet your job and career on this?" and I quickly said, "Absolutely." He turned to one of his guys and told him to make a note of my commitment and we would review it the next year in this same meeting. This comment elicited a sneer in that room full of people, many of whom weren't even peripherally

involved in our decision-making about the shoe business. He was just
an old-school retail jerk with an outsized ego as CEO of a huge corporation, and I could handle that, but the room got very quiet after
our exchange. Was being disrespectful to people below you in a corporation acceptable? Does being a CEO anoint a person with the right
to run roughshod over employees, bullying in front of large groups?
Again, I was way too young to have the answer. I just had the question.
And I pondered that question, along with so many others, in the solitude of airplanes on a regular basis.

Jim Pushes on an Open Door

UPON REFLECTION, THE TIME I spent in department stores was indeed near or at the peak of the life cycle of that sector, just at the tipping point toward a very different future where specialty stores became the dominant channel of distribution for most things sold in department stores, resulting in department stores needing to make moves they would never have considered in the past. But for those moments, things were great indeed. And the rapid growth of north Texas provided the fertile ground that allowed for the spectacular growth Sangers was enjoying. So many incredibly smart retailers came through Sanger-Harris during those years and went on to do terrific things, both in changing department stores and in leading specialty stores. Jim Carreker, Mike Ullman, Kosta Kartsotis, Jim Zimmerman, Don Stone, Linda Knight. The list goes on and on. All became leaders in various positions and industries. It was a privilege for me to spend time there. But it was the time when I got a gnawing feeling in my gut that the future of department stores might hold less opportunities for me than it had in the past.

The stage was set. I was personally firing on all cylinders. A large *Dallas Morning News* article had just appeared focusing on two other young Dallas business executives and me as the rising stars in the Dallas business community. That was the article that pushed Ross Perot to call me the next day to tell me I shouldn't waste any more time at Sanger-Harris. He thought I should start a company and let him be my financial partner.

On a fateful night in the summer of 1982, two years after I joined Sanger-Harris and at the ripe old age of thirty-one, when I had already added other divisions to my Sanger-Harris responsibility and virtually all of my divisions were number one, two, or three in growth percentage across all of FDS, I got a call from my HBS buddy Jim McCurry. He was coming through town and hoping we could get together.

Yes, everything had converged at the same time, which I find amazing. I was pounding a warning drum within Sanger-Harris specifically and Federated Department Stores generally that even as our businesses were great, a real threat to our channel was emerging for the same reason we were expanding, the explosive growth of enclosed regional shopping centers.

With that background, Jim McCurry was going to show me hard data revealing the imminent emergence and potential future explosive growth of a new sector in the entertainment industry. And that entertainment sector had already seen the rapid rise of the record and video industries, resulting in the emergence of specialty record stores and a new specialty chain named Blockbuster Video. Jim was going to teach me about video games and the reasons that the video games sector could be the biggest entertainment sector to date.

Jim was an early partner at Bain. An offer from Bain was an example of the sort of rewards that are offered to students who are named Baker Scholars at HBS. The top 5 percent of graduates earn Baker Scholar recognition. They are courted by virtually every one of the most highly regarded companies in the world. Jim had gone to Bain

Consulting and done extremely well. So when he saw an opportunity to transfer to Bain's new West Coast office where he could target the startups emerging there, he wasted no time replanting himself to California.

What Jim walked me through and showed me visually with charts that evening was stunning and resonated resoundingly with me. He had formally constructed a model for his video game clients in the Silicon Valley that illustrated tangentially what I had been (less eloquently) trying to show the leadership of Sanger-Harris and Howard Goldfeder and the senior executives at Federated Department Stores. While Jim's focus was on the emergence and rapid growth of a new consumer entertainment channel, my focus was on the fact that specialty stores were growing in importance for every category of consumer goods.

Jim described three distinct activities converging to drive this new sector:

1. The growing appetite among younger consumers of all types for new and interesting entertainment formats beyond simple color TVs, portable radios, arcade game machines, and Betamax or VHS movie tapes.

2. The rapid semiconductor chip evolution was yielding chips that were driving down processing times and increasing the amount of information that was being processed. In the case of video games that meant graphic displays of gameplay never before seen with predictions of astoundingly improved graphics in the near future with each new generation of video game machines as semiconductor technology continued its rapid evolution.

3. The advent of new competing electronic formats driven by the technological improvement in chip technology, each fighting for dominance in the new video game sector. That emergence would drive a need for larger assortments of games and

hardware to satisfy the needs of a growing base of users in the face of rapid obsolescence caused by improved semiconductor chip designs.

Based on my newly found realization about the emergence of specialty retailers, I added that if his three points were true, then two retail trends would become inevitable.

1. This demand for larger game software assortments would extend beyond the ability of mass merchandisers to present product in a visually compelling way, which would send customers looking for stores they could count on to have the largest selection of the latest and best games. And this would lead to the emergence of "software" specialty stores that could showcase all software for all formats of existing and emerging video game systems, as well as be the first distribution point for any new hardware system types introduced. The expected rapid price declines for current game formats when new formats were introduced would thus deepen video game penetration into homes across all demographic groups.

2. Finally, semiconductor improvements in sheer amount of computing power coupled with rapidly declining prices for older chips would continue to drive cyclical emergence of newer hardware systems and software that take better advantage of the computing power unleashed by the enhanced semiconductor chips. This would deliver quality content beyond any levels seen before. That virtuous cycle would drive gamers to look for more, better, and faster hardware to power rapidly improving gameplay, and they would then demand more, higher-quality software that showcased the new chips that unleashed faster, greater, and cheaper computing power. As a result, there would be a further proliferation of game titles and formats.

As Jim explained it to me, people had been entertaining themselves since they lived in caves and painted on the walls to express their creativity. And humans have shown their improving creativity in a myriad of ways ever since they left caves. In short, it is evident that entertainment wouldn't go away. Semiconductor technology was simply opening new doors for people to entertain themselves.

Jim was pushing on an open door with me! As Jim was explaining the content piece of his logic, I felt the analogy was perfect—I explained to him that I had been preaching a variation on what he was showing me with little success in the department-store business. Most importantly, as Jim talked about record players, he also pointed out that while the first records in the late 1950s were sold mostly at Sears and JCPenney, ultimately specialty stores selling only records emerged. And large record store specialty chains were beginning to steal market share from the big stores like Sears and JCPenney or superstores like Toys "R" Us. It was pretty obvious to both Jim and me that as the video game industry grew and more titles became available, specialty video game stores would emerge.

Our rationale was clear; as the "installed base" of video game systems grew, the appetite for software to play on the various video game systems would explode, requiring stores to carry broader and broader assortments of games to satisfy customer demand. And if a given store couldn't carry that breadth of product the customer required, the customers would find stores that could. Without a doubt, a specialty-store channel would emerge that carried the broadest and deepest assortments of both video game hardware and software, in locations where the customers congregated with staff who played games themselves and would be able to talk with curious customers and be experts in the business.

I remember becoming very animated as the night wore on at my kitchen table. I was pounding on Jim that he should quit his job at Bain and I would quit my job at Sanger-Harris and we would start a specialty-store retailer that only sold videos games. Just as I felt that Jim was pushing on an open door with me, I felt I was pushing on an open door with him also. Intellectually it was obvious—he and I were in violent agreement about the future and upside for the video game industry—but it was a big step for Jim to consider, as he had a super job making tons of money at a firm he really liked. For me, all I could think about was if Jim would quit his job at Bain to work on this idea, as smart and disciplined as he was, then I would be crazy not to quit my job and join him. Jim would be my insurance policy! By the time the night ended, we were working on names for our new company, although we both knew we were already way over our skis and needed to take a step back and develop a business plan that would support our idea for us to raise money for the venture. So that was our next step, and we both knew there was no rush to quit our jobs, as we could develop the business plan on the side.

While Jim and I were working on our business plan and attempting unsuccessfully to raise funding, we decided to go see Ross. Ross loved that Jim, like Ross, had been in the Navy, so they got along very well. We talked at length about our business idea, explaining that we felt we could open one hundred stores in the first year. He convinced us not to even attempt to open that many stores in year one. Instead, he told us to open one store and run it ourselves until we knew everything a person could know about our stores and then open the second store. He also opined that the two hardest things we would ever do after opening our first store would be to 1) open our second store followed by 2) open our second market. He asked if we needed money, and we told him we really just needed his advice and were raising the money with no issues thus far, although that simply wasn't true. I was also very clear with Ross about not wanting to ruin our relationship if he indeed invested and we lost his money. We thanked him for his advice, which later proved to be fairly close to spot-on, and we left his office.

A couple of months later (by this time we had both quit our jobs and were working full time on our concept while still looking for funding), Jim and I were quite surprised that between the two of our résumés we couldn't find anyone who would share our vision and commit to contributing capital. During that time period, Ross called me late one evening at home. He asked several questions about the business status and whether we had our financing yet. I again told Ross I didn't want his money and that his advice was more important to us than his capital. He then said, and I haven't forgotten his words on that late January 1983 evening, "Well, dammit, it is *my* money, and I can spend it however I want." He asked us to come to his office the next afternoon, where he proposed becoming equal partners with one-third of the equity each: our one-third each was the "sweat," and his one-third was the equity we needed. His sole caveat was that we kept his involvement silent. He was very certain that if it became known that he was our investor, he would become a lightning rod for our company, and he didn't want us to be burdened by his notoriety while we were trying to build a company. That was very wise of him!

Neither Jim nor I was able to quit our jobs quietly—we both received serious pushback from our employers. Jim's took the form of a threat of a lawsuit from Bill Bain, the founder of Bain. He ended up retaining a law firm to sue Jim, but the matter was ultimately settled, though not before I had to go meet Bill Bain for a dinner in New York City, where he pretty firmly made the case for Jim staying in his firm. I responded that Jim was fully capable of making his own career decisions and didn't need Bill or me to tell him what to do. I further commented that working at Bain probably shouldn't be considered indentured servitude, so I found his argument curious. That comment pretty much ended our dinner!

For me, Federated Department Stores was much more insidious in their efforts to keep me. Their first volley was simply to ask if this was a stunt to get a higher salary. After getting my firm no, their second volley was to see if I would stay if I would be named CEO of a division of Federated Department Stores. I was so committed to the new retail specialty-store concept that I told them neither of those thoughts had crossed my mind. They next offered me a $100,000 spot cash bonus just to forget about the idea. When that didn't turn my head, they finally offered me the president's job at Filene's in Boston, which I thought about for a minute and turned down also.

The entire exercise led to a culminating episode in which Howard Goldfeder, the CEO of Federated Department Stores, offered to have his strategic planning team review our business plan. His promise was that if they liked our idea, FDS would be happy to back us in our venture. I happened to know the head of the strategy group at Federated, and several weeks later she tipped me off to the fact that they had reported back to Howard that they thought we might be onto something and that Federated should back us. Much to our chagrin, when Howard called, he told us that our idea was dumb, and we shouldn't do it. His exact words were, "My crystal ball isn't very clear on this, and yours shouldn't be either." Later in my career, when I told that story to Terry Lundgren, by then the great CEO of Macy's, who had indeed systematically shut down the myriad of regionally named old-school department stores and now flew virtually all major department stores in America under the Macy's flag, he became completely frustrated to learn how FDS and Howard had mishandled the opportunity it had to become the equity behind what was by then called GameStop, a global behemoth in a specialty-store sector with a $10 billion market cap.

Jim had committed to moving to Dallas, as he was footloose and I had a growing family, so we began working in Dallas on our new concept. Karleen and I had just had Eric—you can imagine her shock and questions when I suggested that this new specialty-store concept had such upside that we should jump into it with both feet. She politely pointed out that we now had two kids and a big mortgage, and Ben was soon to start kindergarten at a very expensive private school. She knew one of us needed to be the contrarian adult in the room, and it couldn't be me since I had almost jumped into Bill Graham Presents. But she didn't know how hard to push back, as Winterland Productions by that time was already making waves in the music industry, and my friend Don Hunt was doing extraordinarily well in the job her father had me turn down. Karleen ultimately agreed with me that Jim, as smart and as strong a visionary as he was, would be our "insurance policy" on this idea. Little did we know he was sort of thinking the same thing about me as he left one of the most prestigious and highest-paying jobs in America.

Jim and I marveled at how Dallas really rolled out the red carpet for entrepreneurs, and we benefited from that can-do business attitude. Don Zale, then the CEO of Zales jewelry, had become an acquaintance, as Karleen had become very close friends with his daughter Julie when we moved to Dallas. One evening when Don and I were getting to know each other, I described how Jim and I were developing the business model and would be looking for office space shortly. He didn't blink an eye and asked why we wouldn't move into the old Zales jewelry corporate headquarters and pay no rent as long as we wanted to be there. Jim and I were so amazed and jumped at the opportunity. Our first office address was in the legendary Zales jewelry corporate offices, which we both felt was a nice match for us. Over the years, Don and I have cemented our relationship, and he can still kick my rear end on a golf course while being a full fifteen years older than me. He is amazing on so many levels. And Julie and Karleen ultimately started the cookie business together.

I did get one call during those early days in the spring of 1983 that stopped me in my tracks. It was from Stanley Marcus at Neiman Marcus, and by the time he called me he had retired from active management of Neiman's, but he remained involved. At the time of his call, his son Richard had been CEO of Neiman's for perhaps five years. Neiman Marcus was a global retail icon I had grown up with, and it was generally recognized as the nation's finest retailer at the highest end of the market. Growing up in Texarkana, I had looked forward to each Wednesday's *Dallas Morning News*, when Neiman Marcus would run its regular full-page ad. A critical part of that weekly ad was using one column of the ad to showcase customer letters along with "Mr. Stanley's" response. I particularly loved the angry customer letters, realizing that Stanley Marcus was doing something no other stores would dare do: air their dirty laundry by printing letters from customers angry about a Neiman Marcus failure of some sort. My aspirational retail job had been to one day become CEO of Neiman Marcus, and when I joined Carter Hawley Hale stores after HBS at the Emporium division, I had been told that they would not rule out moving me to Neiman Marcus if my results at the Emporium warranted.

My stomach literally flipped when Mr. Stanley, as he was affectionately called by his employees, customers, and the media, introduced himself on the phone. He said he wanted to take me to lunch to talk about Neiman Marcus, as he was helping his son think through a transition to outside management. He had heard many good things about me from several different directions and thought we should know each other. My head and stomach both dropped simultaneously. That had certainly been an aspiration, but given how hard Jim and I were working to get Babbage's off the ground, there was simply no way I could even contemplate jumping off that train before it had started pulling away from the station. With a lump in my throat, I told Mr. Stanley that even if he had questionable enough judgment to want me to consider a role at Neiman Marcus, I would not be able to consider it. He asked me if I was sure, and I said yes. After we hung up, I knew the die was cast for me. Several years later, Terry Lundgren was named CEO of Neiman Marcus. Terry was a far better merchant than I was, and I felt he was straight out of central casting for the Neiman Marcus CEO job and would have won the job over me in all scenarios anyway, so I felt the karma was right all the way around on this one.

Opening the World's First Video Game Store

THERE WAS SO MUCH TO do before the Friday, May 27, of Memorial Day weekend 1983, when the world's first video game store opened for business in NorthPark Center in Dallas, Texas. Jim and I had both quit our jobs by January 1, 1983, and we were working full time on our new concept. This was Jim's and my first effort to actually manage the process of starting a new company, much less opening our first store. Our first task in January of 1983 was to figure out what the store name should be. We pondered names for many hours and did a ton of research. On one end of the spectrum, there were so many concepts already in existence that sold all sorts of games, mostly traditional games like chess, checkers, and Monopoly, but they all had names that started with *game*. There was Game Peddler, Game Zone, Game this, and Game that. We felt we didn't want to drop into an ocean of concepts all with the same word in their name, so we decided not to use *game* in our name. Time has proven that wasn't the best decision. An emerging bookstore concept started in Austin by Gary Hoover called itself Bookstop. While I remember us briefly discussing whether it made sense to think about GameStop, we didn't think long about it. However, Len Riggio, founder of Barnes & Noble bookstores, ultimately bought Bookstop and changed the name of their stores from Bookstop to Barnes & Noble. During the same time period, he also financially backed a company in Minneapolis that started selling video game software a couple of years after we started Babbage's, and he named that concept Software Etc. The third major player that emerged was a company named Electronics Boutique, based in Philadelphia, which had for years sold little handheld electronic games and watches and other items that were electronic in nature but not really video games. As our business grew, both of these concepts began rapid expansion for their own video game assortments also.

Jim and I wrestled hard with names. We thought about going the department-store route and naming it after ourselves. Neither McCurry-Kusin nor Kusin-McCurry made much sense to either of us. We didn't want our names as part of the company name anyway. But we did worry about our concept being so new that no one would understand the word *software*. The thought was that *software* was another word for ladies' underwear, so we ruled that out. That word simply didn't exist to most people in the early 1980s when we started Babbage's, though within a few short years the world would learn what software was as Microsoft emerged, and, not much later, Software Etc.

What we were most worried about at the dawn of the video game era was that people wouldn't understand the power of the new, improved technology and how the video gameplay was so enhanced over past video games due to the powerful new semiconductor chips. While Atari's first home console system had been introduced in 1977, the early Atari game cartridges did not have the memory to deliver great graphics. Other similar second generation systems like the ColecoVision and Mattel Intellivision systems delivered better gameplay than the Atari 2600 and developed followings. Finally, in the fall of 1982, Atari introduced their Atari 5200, a new third generation eight-bit (a measure of memory in the console) video game console, and over the next few years released almost seventy new video games with markedly better graphics than anyone had seen before. The early megahits Pitfall! and Ms. Pac-Man were enormous sellers, along with other new eight-bit third generation console systems like the Nintendo and Sega game systems. The chip wars had begun! There was a proliferation of video game systems, each incompatible with the others and each releasing massive numbers of new games. That was exactly what we had hypothesized would happen. That was how fast the chip technology was improving. The graphics of third generation console systems were leaps (so to speak!) ahead of the Atari 2600 games by the holiday season of 1983. An early game like Pong was all of a sudden made obsolete by the third generation eight-bit semiconductors that opened the door for more robust video game systems and gameplay. Up to that time, the best video gameplay was coming from upright arcade game machines, which were rapidly overtaking pinball machines in the marketplace. Successful arcade games had names like Pac-Man, Frogger, Donkey Kong, Space Invaders, Galaga, and Ms. Pac-Man. All of a sudden, home video game systems were delivering gameplay equal to or better than that of upright arcade machines. In addition, they were introducing home versions of the bestselling upright arcade systems. We felt we had no choice other than to have monitors at the front entrance to our stores that showed repeating loops of gameplay from various home video games we sold. Customers needed to be able to see the high-quality gameplay that was available. That way people could stand out in the mall and watch the monitors without committing to walking through the doors too quickly.

About that same time, a museum in Fort Worth began advertising for a program about the history of computers from their inception to the present. Jim and I quickly drove to Fort Worth and went to the museum and saw a terrific exhibit, complete with the names of people at the dawn of computing. They had names like Norbert Wiener, Lady

Ada Lovelace, and Charles Babbage. We both were attracted to the
name Babbage, as it had a nice, soft feel and was noncontroversial
but might need some explanation. We did serious research on Charles
Babbage and ultimately landed on his name as the name for our company. Charles Babbage was a nineteenth-century mathematician and
entrepreneur in Victorian England. He had invented things like the
cow catcher, which was used on the front of railroad engines to scoop
up and throw cows off of railroad tracks. He had also come up with
the idea for a digital, programmable computer. While he never saw
it come to fruition during his lifetime, he is generally credited with
being the inventor of the computer. He started with what he called the
Difference Engine, which was the first to use the concept of a Jacquard
loom to essentially weave numbers. This led to the development of
what he called the Analytical Engine, which was the first machine
to use punch cards to do the computations. His girlfriend at the time
was Lady Ada Lovelace, Lord Byron's daughter, and she developed the
punch cards. While Charles Babbage is generally known as the father
of hardware, Lady Ada Lovelace is known as the mother of software.
We couldn't consider using her name for our new concept, as there was
a famous porn star at the time whose name was Linda Lovelace, so
that ruled out using Lady Ada's name for our store. Our vision started
coming together: we would make the entire back wall of the store
a giant poster of the Difference Engine, put a plaque at the front of the
store telling the story of Charles Babbage, and add monitors showing
loops of gameplay.

The next big decision Jim and I had to sort out was a conflict res-
olution construct for the two of us. How would we determine a way
forward when an issue arose in which we each had strongly held but
different points of view? After some back-and-forth, we agreed that
we would divide all functional areas of the company, like stores, merchandising, procurement, supply chain and distribution, finance, and
investor relations, between the two of us. Once we were comfortable

with each of our duties and responsibilities, we agreed that if it ever came to a point when we had to vote on an issue, the person responsible for the area of dispute would get two votes. I believe that today, with the benefit of entire careers behind us, Jim would agree that one of our greatest personal achievements was that we never had to have a vote on anything. That is not to say we agreed on everything. We often disagreed on an array of things, from strategic to operational. But when we did disagree, we talked and talked and talked until we both understood the issues, the range of options, and what each thought was the best course of action. And then the one of us with ultimate responsibility would make the call.

The Next Six Stores

OUR FIRST SEVEN STORES WERE all in the Dallas–Fort Worth area. Ross introduced us to Norm Brinker, the well-known founder of Chili's, who gave us so much time to think through the ways we should recruit, train, and compensate the team, and Ralph Rogers, founder of many companies including the national Public Broadcasting Service (PBS), who helped us think strategically about our business model. We opened our first store on May 27, 1983, and true to what we had promised Ross, Jim and I worked the store every hour it was open, either together or one at a time, depending on how busy we were. When Jim wasn't in the store, he was at the office keeping the books. When I wasn't in the store, I was at the office figuring out what the sales indicated about which video game systems were growing the fastest and thus warranted an expanded selection and depth in each title.

We worked the entire schedule seven days a week until mid-September, when a young woman named Mary Evans walked into our store and changed everything. She had heard one of our ads in June for Happy Frogger Day, which had been our Father's Day advertisement. She was the store manager at a local computer store named Compuware and from time to time came to NorthPark Center just to see our store. Mary believed we had a great idea and told us we needed to focus on growth; she would handle the stores for us. Jim formally interviewed her two days later and hired her. From that day forward, Jim made sure that Mary interviewed all prospective candidates for employment. Mary was a University of Iowa graduate and grew from being the first store manager to becoming our first district manager and then to first regional manager and finally to our first head of stores. In her early days at Babbage's, she literally recruited her sorority sisters from the University of Iowa to move to Dallas one at a time to become new store managers. For more than fifteen years, Mary was the glue that held our company together. Soon Babbage's became the number-one recruiter at the University of Iowa, with even more annual hires than IBM, which had previously been the biggest recruiter at Iowa. And Mary was responsible for all of this. We were so lucky she came into our store and into our lives that Friday night in September of 1983. And if she hadn't, Jim and I might have spent a full year managing the first store, as Ross suggested. Ugh! That would have been a huge mistake, and we would have, among other things, given up our first-mover advantage.

By the holiday season of 1983, all seven of our first stores were open, all in the north Texas area. Ross came to each store's grand opening and was always immediately recognized, stopping mall traffic everywhere, which was fun for customers and team members alike. There was a call from Ross to me in April of 1984 that led to Bain Capital and Warburg Pincus buying out Ross's equity and becoming traditional private equity investors in Babbage's.

The switch happened after Ross called me in and told me we might have a problem. Obviously, I was concerned and asked what the problem was. He asked me what revenue we had generated on Saturdays in December at our Valley View store in Dallas. I took out the sales report and gave him the sales for each Saturday in December. He reacted by saying we indeed had a problem. He had been to Valley View the prior

Saturday and found the parking lot filled with cars. When he went into our store, we didn't have the number of customers in the store that we had in December, and this highly concerned Ross. His logic was this— not one more car could park at the Valley View mall parking lot the prior weekend, so there were as many cars at the mall that Saturday in April as there were at the mall in December, yet our sales were much lower in April, which led him to believe that the market was cratering for video games. After trying unsuccessfully to teach him the seasonal impact of Christmas on retail sales, I asked him if he wanted us to find an investor to replace him. He said he didn't want to hurt us, so please take our time, but yes, he would be more comfortable being replaced as an investor.

Jim and I each had personal connections at either Bain Capital or Warburg Pincus. Ernie Pomerantz, a partner at the private equity firm Warburg Pincus, was a cousin of Karleen's who had seen Karleen's father at a Bar Mitzvah in San Antonio. Jack Kaufman gave him the background on Jim, me, Babbage's, and Ross's involvement. Ernie was very interested in getting to know us and our company, so he came to Dallas from New York City, and we showed him what we were doing—bottom line, he let us know that Warburg Pincus would want to invest in Babbage's.

Jim had the same sort of situation at Bain Capital. Jim and Mitt Romney had become friends while each was a partner at Bain Consulting. When Jim peeled off from Bain Consulting to start Babbage's, Mitt had left Bain Consulting to start Bain Capital, a private equity firm that generally was funded by partners at Bain Consulting. Because Jim had worked in the nascent video game industry in Silicon Valley, Mitt already understood the business and was eager to invest in Babbage's also. Mitt came to Dallas to learn about our specific business firsthand, and soon Bain Capital and Warburg Pincus would join forces to buy out Ross Perot. Those two firms became our private equity backers, with Mitt and Ernie each serving as our board members for the next twelve years.

Babbage's Exploding Growth: Negotiating Speed Bumps

THERE WERE SO MANY VARIED experiences in those early years, and they held such great lessons for me. I continued my enormous amount of flying in solitude on airplanes, reflecting on both the differences and similarities between the department stores where I had spent the first six years of my career and what I was seeing now in a budding specialty-store chain. I was always on the lookout for threads that might link together my experiences between department stores and specialty stores and thus give me some advantage. I did come to the conclusion that while each had its own lessons, the overarching strategic principles were the same.

If I had something to say I no doubt would have said it, but at this point in my career, finding the patterns that connected success in large businesses, in start-ups, and over a long career felt a bit like unraveling a Rubik's Cube. I felt there was a unifying pattern to be found at every level of business, not just at a strategic level, but it was eluding me.

A start-up was wildly different from what I had experienced in department stores. Department stores had long histories, and it was easy to find something in their history that informed current actions, at least in the short term. There were playbooks for virtually any eventuality. A sea change in the macro, strategic sense for department stores was much harder to discern, specifically the existential threat of the rise of specialty stores. Specialty stores were quite different. The overarching strategic imperative was very much locked in early in the life of this emerging sector. But the day-to-day issues facing the array of specialty-store start-ups had no historical precedent. There was no playbook. What I was looking for and wondering about was whether or not there might be a set of decision rules that could be relied on to inform a correct course of action for almost anything tactical that could occur in a start-up—as opposed to in a corporate business environment. If so, I would create some tactical decision rules that might contribute to or help inform my strategy-oriented Leadership Principles. But at that time I sensed that the principles were just beyond my reach.

I bet every entrepreneur and start-up has at least one or two crises that amount to life-or-death moments for their companies, and Jim's and my experience at Babbage's was no different. Our biggest existential crisis was the computer inventory management software crisis of 1985. The pain caused for our system was extraordinary. By that time, we were carrying about twelve hundred different video games and other software, each game with its own specific version for each video game system or type of computer. Since none of the video game systems were compatible with any other video game system, we had to carry a separate item for each system. We might carry Ms. Pac-Man as one item for the Sega video game system and another version of Ms. Pac-Man for the Nintendo video game system. So even though both were the same game, Ms. Pac-Man was two separate items in our inventory system. Amazingly, forty years later, each title of video game that is not transmitted to the user digitally still needs to be released on an array of platforms.

Our business was highly seasonal, with virtually all of our annual profits generated in the November, December, and January months. Needless to say, being able to keep all stores stocked with the right titles and video game systems during that peak time period was critically important. Some stores could sell literally hundreds of a single video game in a week if they had enough inventory of that title. It was very tricky to be sure that could happen. It cost lots of money to buy the inventory for the stores, so it was also critical that you buy the right amounts of the right titles and then stock them in correct quantities in each store in order to be profitable. We had software that tracked inventory in each store and projected sales of that inventory, so we felt like we were ready for that holiday season in 1985. We had twenty-three stores open, with others under construction, so our inventory control and management software was already critically important for our young company.

Suddenly, on November 15, out of the blue, our inventory control software crashed. It was truly an existential crisis and resulted in all-hands-on-deck. We soon learned that the software could not be repaired in time for the all-important holiday season. To remedy this disaster, I had to construct a separate manual spreadsheet for each of the twenty-three stores. On each spreadsheet for each store, I listed our top one hundred items as a company and then left room for up to ten items not in the top one hundred that any particular store could ask to be replenished also. I set a personal schedule to call each store manager at their home each night when their store closed, after they had counted their top one hundred items inventory and computed how many they had sold of each title on that specific day. I would be sitting at my home kitchen table with an extra-long extension cord for the phone. As I spoke to each manager, I would write in their sold and on-hand amounts for each of the top one hundred items plus whatever other items they wished. Once I had that information from all twenty-three stores—several hours' work each night, seven nights a week for eight weeks—I would manually generate "pick tickets" for each item for each store, and then the next day in our distribution center we would pick, pack, and ship the needed software directly to each store.

It was a nightmare of the highest order, and after the holiday season passed Jim and I determined that we would get an expert to write a comprehensive inventory control and management software program for us to use going forward. And to make sure it could handle our future needs, we had it built to handle up to ten thousand stores and ten thousand software items, which seemed a ridiculous requirement for a company with thirty stores, but we were nothing if not aspirational! We developed the software and called it BRIAN (Babbage's Retail Inventory Allocation Network). Over thirty years later, in 2015, long after Jim and I had left Babbage's and it had become GameStop, with a large global footprint, I learned that all six thousand plus stores around the world continued to use BRIAN for managing inventory. The fun ending to that story is that no one at GameStop had a clue what BRIAN stood for or the history of the software. But they still called it BRIAN nevertheless. Alas, in 2023 GameStop announced that one of its top initiatives going forward was to update its inventory control and management software. Not bad, an almost-forty-year run by BRIAN!

Another interesting outgrowth of that episode is that the person we hired to write the new BRIAN software at the time, a very young man named Scott Lipsky, became a world-famous entrepreneur in his own right after creating the BRIAN software for Babbage's. He went on to become CTO for companies like Barnes & Noble, but his big claim to fame is that he and Jeff Bezos met in 1996, and not long thereafter, Jeff asked Scott to become the first VP of Business Expansion for Amazon, when it was an infant. Obviously, that became the fastest business expansion in history. Since then, Scott has gone on to become, among many other things, a Hollywood producer and investor. Good on you, Scott!

Our rate of growth, combined with a very young and inexperienced team learning on the fly how to deal with the array of issues that surfaced, led to a very strong culture at Babbage's. We felt like we were on a mission to create the best video game stores in the world. "We were fearless," is how Opal Ferraro, our CFO, described it recently, and I think that is a great descriptor. There was such fabulous alignment across the company with what we were trying to do. And all the while I was making mental notes while staring out the airplane windows!

Every company is in favor of "a great culture." It is almost axiomatic. But actually finding companies with great cultures is very hard. I believe a great culture is a result of doing a lot of other things right. It includes everyone being aligned on what the aspirational goal is for a company. It also includes giving team members the tools they need to deliver the results they promise. Too often there is responsibility without authority. And that leads to bad cultures. Rewards, recognition, and celebration are clues that a great culture exists. When I visit with new companies, I love asking how they celebrate successes. It tells a lot. I was starting to put it all together, beginning with the realization that although companies all over the world like to point to their cultures as their key strength, that is simply incorrect. Culture, again, is a result of a strong set of principles or a vision that unites an organization behind a set of goals and informs what behaviors are and are not acceptable within that organization. And then that culture can be seen every day in every way as the company moves forward.

Building a Great Culture
with "Culture Carriers"

TODAY I CALL TEAM MEMBERS known for living the Leadership Principles within a company the Culture Carriers. These are people who consistently find reasons and ways to model behaviors not just consistent with—but underscoring and exemplifying—the start-up and vision being developed. The behavior can be modeled through celebration events, rewards or recognition, and individuals presenting a consistency of character or style that maps to the aspirational goals of the organization. A good example of celebration and what it reveals about culture is the prank Jim once pulled on a new district manager as he was promoting him. Mark Mellecker was one of the Iowa graduates whom Mary Evans recruited to come to Babbage's. Though Mark graduated from Iowa, he was a big-time Indiana basketball fan, especially of Bob Knight, the famous coach of Indiana's men's basketball team at the time. Besides the fact that he had won a national championship, Coach Knight was famous for his hair-trigger temper and even had been known to throw his folding chair onto the basketball court at times during games when he was particularly mad at a referee, an opponent, or one of his own players. Jim always teased Mark about how he could have such passion for such a volatile coach as Coach Knight, but Mark could give as well as he got from Jim. When it was time for Jim to promote Mark to district manager of our newest district in Houston, Jim flew down to Houston to offer Mark the job. But he had planned a great practical joke. He met Mark in the Willowbrook Babbage's store, which Mark managed, known for its huge back room. Jim started by telling Mark that the Willowbrook store looked awful, and he couldn't believe how Mark could have allowed it to get so run down. As he talked Jim's voice got louder and louder until he picked up a chair and tossed it across the floor. Mark's eyes were as big as silver dollars, and he didn't know what to say. Then Jim told Mark he was just practicing up for how he would supervise Mark since he was going to name him the Houston district manager. You can only imagine what a deep breath Mark exhaled when he realized what was happening. Chalk one up for Jim and one for Mark for being able to take a classic joke! But behind that great practical joke was trust— these two people trusted each other and liked each other. Only where there is trust can a practical joke not have repercussions later. More importantly, in our young company everyone knew Jim and everyone knew Mark. Everyone *loved* that Jim had successfully and hysterically pranked Mark because Mark never stopped talking about his love for all things Bob Knight. People really enjoy being part of a company where people know how to have fun while still working very hard. At Babbage's, everyone felt aligned on the importance of the culture we were building. And trust abounded within the company.

Another much more telling story about the unique culture we built at Babbage's came from our finance organization. Opal Ferraro was our CFO for the most time during our tenure. She was working at Arthur Young, at that time a Big Eight accounting firm, when we reached out to her. She had just been promoted to principal at Arthur Young and had a great career path laid out for herself there. But she agreed to come interview with Jim, which led to other interviews across the company and our offering her the CFO role. Opal recently told me that in spite of Babbage's only having sixteen stores when she joined and our losing money due to our rapid growth, she had never seen such an exciting company, brimming with energy. Years later, when Babbage's was much bigger and Opal was worried about our 3 percent inventory shrinkage, she retained a firm that only conducted shrinkage audits to learn if there was an inventory loss problem due to theft and, if so, what remediation could be done to mitigate the shrinkage level. After all, we were selling the most sought-after products to millions of customers across America.

Opal retained the firm, and their initial report was telling. Our inventory loss each year was running around 3 percent. The firm's audit suggested that due to the category of inventory we sold and how we displayed it, they would have expected the shrinkage to be 8 percent, significantly higher than the 3 percent reported. They were most concerned about how it was that our systems suggested a 3 percent shrinkage when their projection had been almost three times that number. They offered to do a deep dive to pressure test our systems because they were quite sure the shrinkage was much more than was being reported, which would be a big problem if true. We approved their new project because we wondered if indeed our shrinkage was closer to 8 percent. When they came back with their final audit report, they reported that indeed our inventory shrinkage was 3 percent. They had done extensive interviewing throughout the company and reported that they had never seen as cohesive a culture as existed at Babbage's. They said that everyone acted like owners, and no one would ever let anything bad happen to the inventory. That was a terrific insight in its own right. We held people accountable. Most importantly, we gave them the authority that matched their responsibility. We hadn't realized what a breakthrough that was. Responsibility to match authority and then accountability for the responsibility we had given to team members. The seeds for my later Leadership Principles were hiding in plain sight! The inventory audit firm was truly astounded. I suppose Jim, Opal, and I were also, but we were just like our other team members. We each loved the company and would never have let anything bad happen to its inventory either.

People promote and model what behaviors are most aligned with the aspirations of a company. In business start-ups at the outset, it is best to staff with "unicorns"—people who are multitalented and can do whatever is necessary each day to keep the company moving forward. Unicorns must be utility players, doing whatever they are called on to do.

Mary Evans wasn't our only unicorn. We had several to start, and that grew into many. But Terri Yerant was special among the unicorns. Another Midwesterner who found her way to us through existing team members, she first worked in our stores and soon became a store manager. But as our need for merchants grew, we threw her into the role of becoming our first buyer. She not only was stellar while learning the ropes of merchandising, she developed a reputation in the market as an astute selector of product who had high integrity, broad intellect, and an infectious laugh. She represented Babbage's well in the marketplace, and over the years she built a superb merchant group led by Doreen Erickson, which continued to rise to the occasion as Babbage's grew and our operations became more complex. Doreen became the lead buyer for GameStop and retired from that role over twenty years later.

As companies mature, they require more "subject matter experts," people who have trained in one area, built expertise, and know how to stay in their own lane to create the most value. And Babbage's quickly grew to the stage where we needed some deep subject matter expertise rather than just unicorns. But these subject matter experts had to have the character and the characteristics to become Culture Carriers within Babbage's. Opal was an example of a subject matter expert; she had deep experience in finance and brought that with her when she joined us. Ron Freeman was another such talent. To this day

I have never worked with an executive quite like Ron Freeman. Having strong and successful prior work experience at the Gap, Ron ran all of our supply chain, distribution, logistics, and ultimately any project we needed done right. Besides being a world-class human being in every way, Ron was an outstanding executive, team leader, and teacher. I recently had a two-hour lunch with Ron, catching up about what was happening with him in his life and reminiscing about Babbage's and GameStop. A perfect example of his burning desire to be the best came to light when he discussed an aspect of his work during the time after we had changed our name to GameStop. He explained in great depth how he had driven the total cost of handling a game in the distribution center down by over 77 percent across tens of millions of video games in a year. Imagine the cost savings Ron brought with that initiative alone. Now multiply that across all his areas of responsibility. It is absolutely astounding by any measure. But that was Ron. I will never forget the year I didn't give Ron an Outstanding grade on his annual review. I don't remember the reason, but it must have been sufficient, probably something related to overall company results, as I knew it wouldn't sit well with Ron. I surely hope it was a good reason because even today, no doubt, Ron still remembers that annual review. He was completely dejected, almost depressed. He had never, *ever*, in his career gotten anything other than the highest ranking available. I didn't doubt that, though I hadn't known it. If we worked together ten years, for nine of them he scored Outstanding, a score reserved for the top 5 percent of the entire team each year. As I tried to explain to Ron at the time, in a ten-year career the averages suggest an employee would score Outstanding perhaps once. He eventually got over it, but it was very hard for him. Even today I smile when I think about Ron— any task he was given, even those close to impossible to achieve, he would receive it with a smile and then get it done. He was a one-man gang in the distribution center: teaching, cajoling, teasing, advancing systems, and modeling behaviors that would lead to success for all in his area. And then he would wander into the office and do the same thing. He was beloved across the company, and people stepped up their game just because he would walk by. He engendered respect for his competency, his attitude, and his results. And in his downtime during the lunch hour, he would lift weights in the warehouse. I had not seen a more physically fit person. And his muscle cars in the parking lot were as tough and durable as he was.

Culture Carriers sometimes come from the most unlikely places. I handled most of the early leases at Babbage's and knew we needed a professional as we grew, but I couldn't find anyone who not only had impeccable real estate credentials but also would be a great cultural fit. And the Babbage's culture was so important to maintain since we were growing explosively. Then one day my phone rang and a big voice on the other end announced himself as E. K. Spieckerman, the ex-head of real estate from Radio Shack. He had personally completed something like six thousand leases for Radio Shack and for many years had reported directly to Charles Tandy, founder and CEO of Tandy Corporation, the parent company of Radio Shack. E. K. had retired from Radio Shack and was itching to go back to work. His was the largest personality at Babbage's during his tenure, and he was by far the oldest person in the company, yet he had such a physically imposing presence. People across Babbage's loved when he was in the building. His booming voice and raucous laugh could be heard throughout the halls. And he worked so hard and was held in such complete awe by the real estate community. I couldn't help but notice that when I traveled with E. K. into the real estate market, the CEOs of the major real estate companies we visited attended the meetings, and it was always like a reunion. E. K. would grab the CEOs, lift and hug them, and immediately remind them of some funny anecdote from the past. E. K. was a large man, well over six feet tall, burly, and with flyaway bushy gray eyebrows. And he couldn't simply walk up a flight of stairs. He *always* took two stairs at a time, so I would get a workout just trying to keep up with him in the market. I so enjoyed the meetings when we were together in front of people like the DeBartolo family or Mel Simon. These developers were among the biggest, best, and toughest mall developers in America. And while the founders and owners of major national real estate firms seldom, if ever, met with small companies, they all knew when E. K. was arriving and spent quality time with him in their offices. And somewhere along the line you could count on E. K. standing up and bellowing, in the heat of negotiating a rent rate with a landlord, "Hell, I don't want to buy the space, I just want to lease it!" We had our greatest store opening expansion with E. K. leading the way.

But culture development doesn't happen seamlessly or without speedbumps as it develops. There are missteps and lapses of judgment. I was guilty of one that I have taught in MBA ethics classes for over twenty years. Barry Fehrs was our head of construction at Babbage's. At the time he was in his early thirties. We were opening stores at an accelerating rate, and Barry was charged with getting them all open on time and within budget. That was it—only two responsibilities. That was his entire job description. I remember like yesterday when Opal walked into my office and wanted to know what to do about an expense reimbursement form submitted by Barry that included four tires for a bass fishing boat trailer that cost $800. I scratched my head and called Barry into my office and asked about the charge. He told me that a building inspector in Cleveland had told him to get the tires or he would red-tag our store, meaning that he would say the store doesn't pass the city inspection so it couldn't open. And he would find a reason to continue red-tagging the store until he got his tires. Barry, knowing he was being paid for on-time and on-budget store openings, did what he needed to do to hit his goals. He bought the inspector his tires. He wasn't hiding anything—he had filed for an expense reimbursement. Barry was being 100 percent transparent. But I knew paying off an inspector was wrong, as did our CFO, and I didn't want that to be an acceptable business practice. But I wasn't sure what to do. Barry was correct—I had repeatedly told him he had two objectives and two only. I felt culpable along with Barry. It was a huge lesson for me about honesty and integrity, and it stuck with me through the rest of my career. At the end of the day, I told Barry he would have to pay the $800 himself, as it was illegal to pay bribes, and we couldn't be in that business. He understood and took his medicine, though I have to admit that I also overpaid his bonus that year by $800 due to my guilt at not being specific enough. It kept coming back to me—Barry didn't try to hide or disguise what he had done. You simply wouldn't believe how emotional MBA students get on both sides of this issue when I talk about it in classrooms today.

Babbage's was a formative experience for me on so many levels. That situation with Barry was a good example. I had a great respect for the notion that it is hard to see around corners. But I couldn't make that an excuse, even though it certainly would have applied in this instance. Or I could lean on the adage that while some people are "ready, aim, fire" types of personalities, always thinking and planning ahead, others, like me, were more "ready, fire, aim," which can often lead to shooting yourself in the foot. But that couldn't be an excuse for an ethical lapse either. I had learned the power of alignment and accountability, creating a company where people enjoyed their work, leaned into their work, and took great pride in the results of their work. But this episode taught me that since it is often impossible to see around corners, the intentions should all be built on a foundation of honesty and integrity. If nothing else, it is a catchall that can be used to lead thinking through consequences when something new but unacceptable occurs.

Babbage's became one of the largest video game sellers in America, along with Walmart and Toys "R" Us. So we had relationships with the top software publishers in the industry. I am most proud of the relationship we had with Electronic Arts (EA), from its founder Trip

Hawkins to its longtime CEO Larry Probst and so many others in EA. We felt they were the best publisher and believed they felt we were the best specialty operators. We were connected in so many ways across the years that it is no surprise that our relationship was as strong as it was. They were the earliest video game publisher to understand that packaging would be critical in the future of the video game industry. Prior to their launch, most of EA's competitors were simply putting their software in baggies and shipping it into the retail channel in those baggies. Truly, they would buy a box of baggies like the Ziploc bags used today. A floppy disk in a plastic bag. EA understood marketing and the critical importance of the product standing out on the shelf amongst a myriad of other titles. Now imagine any major record album being launched in the same period. The record covers were full color, with highly stylized, imaginative graphics on the album covers, front and back. From their very launch, each item in the Electronic Arts product lineup shipped like a record, in that it arrived in the same kind of highly stylized record album type cover. Not a single video game publisher came close to their packaging for years. And the very first shipment of product in Electronic Arts history was to a little retailer in Dallas named Babbage's to display in Babbage's first store on its first day in business! The connection between EA and Babbage's literally goes back to day one for both companies. And to put a finer point on that, the day I walked out of Babbage's on February 1, 1995, I stepped onto the Electronic Arts board of directors. While I spent twelve spectacular years at Babbage's, from 1983 until 1995, I spent fifteen years on the EA board of directors and consider that the most important and fun board assignment in my career. EA was every bit as much an academy company as PepsiCo, IBM, GE, or FedEx were in their sectors. It was simply the best-managed video game company in the marketplace. They had a culture based on innovation, and they rewarded innovators. Because they grew so quickly, they always had openings in the organization and preferred to promote from within.

If you distinguished yourself with results, you were rewarded. They were generous with their incentives, and many, many employees built significant net worth over their careers at EA.

I was beginning to think it might make sense to formalize and talk about those principles we were recognizing as critical parts of the success of Babbage's. The problem was I had no real model of a set of principles in any company I had been involved with. But I was learning during the Babbage's days that guiding principles could come from things a company did well as well as from things that were done incorrectly. Paying a bribe to a city inspector in Cleveland is a great example. But I had so simplified the goals and objectives that I left lots of wriggle room. Honesty and integrity would have to be in bright lights when I got around to truly codifying and then speaking about Leadership Principles. And it didn't come from being axiomatic in any setting. The Cleveland problem came about because certain principles weren't discussed, and in a rapid growth environment with very narrow objectives and lots riding on success, it became easy to look past something so mission critical. I was trying to think about strategic versus tactical goals and which type should rise to the surface. This was all new to me, but it was something I was developing a passion for, and I had hundreds of hours on airplanes to reflect. I had lots percolating, with no real idea about how to unify and codify the thoughts I had. That would come with more experiences!

Key Lessons

PART 4

Embrace the Trendsetters:

Seek out and align with innovative thinkers within your industry. Their energy isn't just invigorating—it's contagious and can elevate your own performance.

Numbers Lead the Way:

Adopt a data-driven approach in your decision-making. Let metrics illuminate the subtleties and nuances that can refine your business strategy.

Cultivate Your Network:

When you witness excellence elsewhere, reach out. A conversation with a peer excelling in your field can unlock new avenues for growth.

Strategic Agility Is Key:

Recognize and adapt to the shifting landscapes of your industry. The rise of specialty stores teaches us to stay nimble and be ready to pivot for sustained success.

Inventory Wisdom:

Understand and implement GMROI. It's not just about having inventory; it's about having the right inventory and turning it over efficiently.

Celebrate Your Team's Successes:

Build a culture in which achievements are recognized.
A team that shares in success is a team that strives for it.

Learn from Every Role:

Every position offers a chance to hone skills and absorb new
insights. Tackle each task with the intent to learn and grow.

Mentorship Matters:

Be proactive in your learning. Reach out to those who excel,
and don't shy away from offering wisdom to others.

Dive into the Data:

Utilize resources like *The Red Book* to benchmark your
performance against the industry's best. This isn't about
competition; it's about setting a bar for your own progress.

Power of Culture:

Cultivate an environment in which everyone is invested in
the company's success. When your team acts like owners,
remarkable results follow.

Transparency Builds Trust:

Clarity and openness will foster trust and respect, in
negotiations, in planning, and in every aspect of your work.

Find the Courage to Innovate:

Lead by example in embracing new concepts and tools. Be
the first to adopt, adapt, and innovate.

Elevate Your Vision:

Don't just manage; lead with a visionary approach. It's not
enough to fill the floor space; aim to fill a gap in the market.

PART FIVE

LEADERSHIP PRINCIPLES EMERGE

My Decision to Leave Babbage's

I HAVE LOVED THE SONG "Ooh La La" by Faces since it was released. I think it's because of the lyrics of the chorus: "I wish that I knew what I know now when I was younger." By 1994 Jim and I were grappling with a way to move forward. We were over eleven years into our time at Babbage's, and we felt like we needed a strategic reset, but neither of us quite knew how to do that. We were both in our early forties at this point and likely victims of our own success—we dominated the specialty-store sector in our space and were publicly traded and generally well liked by our investors. We believed in our DNA that we had cracked the code for operating in the world of video games, and our results suggested that was correct.

More importantly, Jim and I were wrong or had just missed two key facts that were impacting our market and creating the next leg of growth that we could have taken. Eleven years after opening our first store in NorthPark, we continued to believe that enclosed regional malls were the only place we could generate the sales numbers we needed for profitability and have a venue with customers wealthy enough to be able to afford the high prices of video games. That was simply wrong. Secondly, average video game prices had not come down in eleven years, though obviously inflation had helped make the price tag of games more palatable to the vast audience of gamers. But we still felt game buying required a wealthier customer.

We were wrong about both of those assumptions. Major enclosed regional malls were giving way to "power centers," outdoor shopping centers with big superstores as their anchors. They were taking serious market share from the enclosed regional malls where we operated, and we missed the opportunity those new outdoor centers could present us for store locations. Not only could we open stores for a lot less capital due to the lack of design requirements in outdoor centers, we also would have lower rents than those in the very expensive enclosed malls, which would mean lower break-even revenue requirements for those locations. Additionally, had we begun opening outside of enclosed malls, it also would have given us a potential way to change our name, which we had a gut feeling should be changed to something that was more appropriate now that the world understood video games and what the word "software" meant. Finally, we completely missed the fact that because of the sustained high video game pricing, a new and enormous market would emerge for buying and selling used video games and refurbished video game systems. To add insult to injury, we knew the person who was starting just such a company, named FuncoLand. We did have conversations about buying that company, but the $5 million price tag seemed unrealistic to us. It turns out that had we acquired his company for the $5 million he asked, that price would have been right up there with the Louisiana Purchase in value! Years later, after GameStop had bought FuncoLand for close to $100 million, used and refurbished software and video game systems generated most of GameStop's profits, close to $500 million annually.

But there was an even bigger strategic principle that we had both missed and that I swore I would not again. That is the notion of continuous improvement. All companies have life cycles. Everyone knows that. But the notion that continuous improvement is the life-blood of a company is critical. It can inform actions. It brings its own energy. For years in the future, I told my various companies that I get most nervous when things are going great. After all, today's peacock becomes tomorrow's feather duster! And at this point in my career, when business is best is when I pop the hood of the car and start tinkering with the engine. Good business can be paralyzing. Everyone freezes, not wanting to do anything to slow things down or cause something unforeseen. But the time for change is precisely when things are going best. Jim and I both missed that, and that is probably the key learning from Babbage's. Virtually every thought we had at the start, from why we picked regional enclosed malls to the reason we adopted the unusual Babbage's name and very different store fixturing and design were for reasons that were right at the time we made the decision. But those reasons gradually lost their significance, and we should have rethought our strategy. This idea of the requirement for constant improvement needed more reflection, but it felt very much like a principle that would serve any company in any industry at any stage of its life cycle.

Jim and I, frustrated as we were, fell back into the strategic thought that there needed to be a roll-up of the three biggest players in the video game specialty-store space to develop additional market pricing power and leverage to take us to the next level. The three largest players in 1994 were Babbage's, Software Etc., and Electronics Boutique. We felt we were the right company to roll up the other two, as we were public with access to capital and were generally regarded in the industry as the best operators. Jim and I were arguing about the best way forward more than we were being smart, and we both felt that was unsustainable and unhealthy for our relationship. Jim offered to step back into a strategic role and have me take over more of the operations, which I didn't think was very smart, as Jim had all the relationships with Wall Street. Plus, Jim was highly integrated into many areas of operations where I felt he was mission critical. And while I really loved our merchant, distribution, and real estate organizations, which were my major areas of oversight, I felt they could do just as well without me.

I began thinking about what my personal go-forward options might be. I also felt like I was more open to changing my career direction than Jim might be, so I raised my antennae and opened my strategic aperture wider than I ever had before. I was smarter from the eleven entrepreneurial years I had spent than I had been before we started and was thinking another start-up might benefit from my Babbage's experience. During this same time period, Terry Lundgren, my old friend from the early days at Federated Department Stores, had moved to Dallas to become CEO of Neiman Marcus. Terry and his family lived about six blocks from us, and we were both in the Dallas Young Presidents' Association chapter. Because of our long-standing friendship and love for department-store retailing we would go to lunch periodically just to stay up on each other's progress. At these lunches I would ask Terry what was going on new and different in the world of high-end specialty stores. After many lunches over several years and not hearing much new or exciting that might catch my attention, I perked up when Terry came to a lunch in late 1993 or early 1994 very excited about MAC cosmetics, which stood for Makeup Artist Cosmetics, a company from Canada that was experiencing explosive growth at cosmetics counters around the world. The sales they were generating were phenomenal—almost unbelievable. Additionally, the Bobbi Brown line was experiencing almost that same level of growth at Neiman's. As he described MAC, Bobbi Brown, and then Trish McEvoy and others, I started thinking about what Terry was saying through the prism of my cosmetics experience at Sanger-Harris. An "opportunity" light flashed on in my head! I had it on my mental back-burner, but it continued flashing. I wasn't sure enough about it to speak with Jim, but it was percolating.

Len Riggio Has a Dream,
and We Lose Our Breakfast!

IT WAS 1994. I WAS forty-three years old and feeling certain I could jump to the next entrepreneurial idea and leave Babbage's in good hands, so I began to work hard to make an acquisition happen. We learned through the market that the founder of Electronics Boutique, James Kim, was not interested in a sale at any price. And he was on his way to becoming a billionaire, so we believed him and focused on Software Etc. as the likely company we should buy. It was based in Minnesota and by this time had Barnes & Noble as its corporate owner. The founder and CEO of Barnes & Noble, Len Riggio, had become a financial backer of Software Etc. and ultimately the controlling shareholder. We knew Dick Fontaine and Dan DeMatteo, the top two people at Software Etc., and felt they were good businesspeople also, so we started making overtures to the company. Ultimately Len Riggio came to Dallas and spent a couple of days with Jim and me. We toured his Barnes & Noble stores, and he explained how they made real estate decisions. We felt that we could make good progress on a deal, especially since Len had assured us he would be able to convince Dick and Dan that even though they would both lose their jobs in a consolidation, it was the right next step for Software Etc. Unfortunately, Len came back to us and said that Dick and Dan weren't interested, as it meant their company would have to shut down Minneapolis, and most of their staff would lose their jobs. At that time, he really started pushing the idea of making it not an acquisition but a merger of equals, which would be helpful with optics at Software Etc. A "merger of equals" means that one company doesn't buy the other but that the two companies merge. He continued to promise that it wasn't about Dick and Dan losing their jobs and that he would move Dick and possibly also Dan into his Barnes & Noble company in any scenario. But I knew that any way they cut it, and no matter what they said, it was all about Dick and Dan losing their jobs.

After consultations with our board of directors, we went back to Len with a proposal that the combination could be a merger of equals, with the only firm requirement on our side being that the new company would be based in Dallas. We further agreed that we would take their best Software Etc. employees into positions in the combined entity, as we would need a larger workforce for the new, almost-twice-as-large company. They came back saying that we also needed a new name, as they couldn't stomach using the name Babbage's on a combined company, which Jim and I were certainly sympathetic to. We quickly agreed to develop a new name for the combined company. It appeared that we had a deal, and we set about getting the paperwork done. During the morning of the closing date, as we were signing documents at our lawyer's office in downtown Dallas, we got a call from Len. He claimed that he "had a dream that the merger wouldn't work," and his wife told him if he dreamt it then he should act on it. He called off the deal, even as we were finishing signing the final documents. Jim and I were aghast. Len Riggio had a dream, and the business combination of the two biggest players in the video game software world was dead! Our esteem for Len dropped through the floor.

At our next board of directors meeting, we all started by commiserating about the failed merger of equals. I continued to press the belief that this was all about Dick and Dan not wanting to lose their jobs. The board seriously doubted that was the case, so I asked permission to pursue that line of logic on my own with Dan since I was sure Len would hire Dick for Barnes & Noble but less sure he would hire Dan.

Since our founding, Jim had been chairman, and I had been president. We didn't use the title CEO, as we both believed in our partnership. My idea was that if I could get Dan to accept Jim as chairman and CEO, he could become president of the combined entity, which would still be located in Dallas. He would have to move, but it would be for a bigger job at the combined company, and his ego would be satisfied by how it played out. I called Dan on the phone and asked if he would meet me at the airport in St. Louis, as I had an idea to present him. We both agreed to that meeting, and in the St. Louis airport I laid out the plan. He agreed that it made perfect sense to combine the companies. I told him that I was an entrepreneur and if he could get his head around Jim being CEO and himself moving to Dallas as president, he could help oversee the merger, and I would go start another company. At the end of the meeting, Dan assured me that he and Dick would never have killed the deal just because they would lose their jobs and that they were only trying to do the right thing for their company. He confirmed that Len indeed did have a dream, which continues to this day to cause me to scratch my head. And without any firm commitment, Dan said he would think about it and get back to me.

Within a week he called me back and told me he would agree to move to Dallas as president and that, yes, Len had agreed to move Dick into Barnes & Noble. He clearly had talked with Len and worked through all the Software Etc. personnel issues. We had a deal! After Jim became comfortable that I was leaving to pursue a new start-up (vintage Jim—making sure I was OK before he thought about himself!) and with his new CEO position over both of the companies, he was satisfied and knew that this gave the newly combined company the size leverage to push the company further into new growth. We called our board, and that started the last lap into a new career for me, a new name for the more powerful combined company, a new title for Jim, and a new job for Dan DiMatteo. It felt right for all constituencies of both firms and all team members. The combined companies came up with a new corporate name, NeoStar Retail Group, which later became GameStop.

Everything Old Is New Again: Cofounding Laura Mercier

THOUGH I WAS STILL WORKING at Babbage's, here is how my mind was spinning by mid-1994: I was thinking about the new makeup artist cosmetics trend in the context of the history of the cosmetics industry and my potential reimmersion in it. When I began my stint at Sanger-Harris in 1980, I had responsibility for all cosmetics in addition to children's merchandise, women's accessories, and all jewelry. As part of my merchandising duties back then, I had studied the cosmetics industry's evolution through very different cycles since the advent of professionally run cosmetics companies in the 1930s and 1940s. The first phase of retail cosmetics growth was driven by makeup artists whose names included Estée Lauder, Princess Marcella Borghese, the Revson brothers of Revlon fame, and others. They all derived their credibility through their work with Hollywood's glamorous stars of the era, like Marlene Dietrich and Greta Garbo, along with fashion models of the day. The women who applied their makeup generated huge credibility among the general population as experts, and the movie stars were examples to the public of what they could look like if they only had the makeup that the great makeup artists were creating and using.

While the first makeup firm in the world was actually Shiseido in Japan, this new generation of makeup artists all began to market their own products, and thus was born Revlon (1934), Lancôme (1935), Estée Lauder (1946), and lines like Borghese (1957). Customers were excited to have access to the makeup that made the movie stars and fashion models look so beautiful. The next stage of evolution for cosmetics was driven by technological innovations in the chemistry of cosmetics. Suddenly there were lipsticks that stayed on all day, powders that did the same, and skin care regimens approved by laboratories or lab developed. Customers flocked to these types of companies, like Clinique (1968). Finally, as retail branding increased in importance, couture fashion apparel lines put out their own cosmetics lines aligned with their most current fashions. So you might see a Chanel cosmetics advertisement showing the color red as "the fashion color for fall" on a model who was wearing Chanel fashions. Even if customers might not be able to afford the couture fashion apparel, they could stretch to buy that red lipstick.

It struck me that the oldest form of selling cosmetics had become new again in the mid-1990s. Not since the start of cosmetics retailing had makeup artists been treated as an entirely new reason to buy cosmetics. Yet here they were—MAC, Bobbi Brown, and Trish McEvoy all trumping the fashion-oriented brands and the technology-focused brands. It felt to me that this was the next wave that would drive the cosmetics industry forward. Since I potentially would need to think about business after Babbage's, this felt like a possible next opportunity, so I pushed hard on the idea.

I talked with Terry Lundgren about my idea to launch a new cosmetics line led by a makeup artist. Terry had left Neiman Marcus in mid-1994 to return to Federated Department Stores, where he ultimately became chairman and CEO. Because Jim and I had had such a strong relationship as partners and cofounders of Babbage's, I was thinking about who might be a good cofounder to join me. Terry thought the cosmetics idea was great and that maybe I should contact Janet Gurwitch, who I had met at a party at Terry's home months before. Janet had been head of merchandising at Neiman Marcus when Terry was CEO, and Terry thought she might be helpful as a cofounder in the start-up. She could be our face of the company, while I financed the company and worked behind the scenes on operations activities. I invited Janet to lunch and quickly began talking about MAC cosmetics. I laid out my thesis about the history of the cosmetics industry and my belief that the original makeup artist trend from forty to fifty years past was making a strong resurgence, which led to an opportunity. I told her that I felt with her fashion leadership capabilities and my capital and entrepreneurial experience, we should make a run as cofounders starting a new company in the makeup artist space. Janet had reservations at first, but once I told her I was going to do it with or without her, she was all in. I used the same construct Ross Perot had used with us at Babbage's. She would get a third of the company for her involvement, I would get a third of the company for my involvement, and the financial backer (also me) would get a third of the company. Janet was happy being president, and I became the chairman and CEO.

Kusin Gurwitch Cosmetics, LLC, was incorporated in Delaware early in 1995, and we filed for our first lipstick trademarks on November 2 and November 3, 1995. I borrowed $3 million on margin in early 1995, using my Babbage's stock as collateral, and the company was born. Janet quit her job at Neiman's and jumped in with both feet. She took care of the sales and product development side of the business, and I concerned myself with the finance, manufacturing, logistics, and IT parts of the business.

Janet had an inspired idea for finding the best available makeup artist in the industry who could guide us in the development of our line of cosmetics. She contacted the fashion editors of the top fashion magazines, which at the time were *Vogue, Harper's Bazaar, Allure, Seventeen,* and *Mademoiselle.* She asked each of the five beauty editors who were the top three makeup artists in the world at the moment. There were two or three names on each list. I remember only two— Kevyn Aucoin and Laura Mercier. We interviewed each of them as well as some other names that came through various third parties, and we thought the answer was obvious. Laura Mercier was the only person with a definite point of view about cosmetics and how she would approach developing a line. At the time, she was doing makeup for top global celebrities like Madonna. Janet and I both liked her but agreed she would be a handful to manage. Janet was up for the challenge, so we developed a license agreement with Laura. We would pay for her to develop a line of cosmetics, since neither Janet nor I had the background, skill set, or experience to develop one. We would develop the packaging and marketing and sales efforts, and Laura would be paid a royalty based on sales. We were now in business with our new makeup artist line: Laura Mercier Cosmetics. We had successfully cofounded a makeup artist–driven cosmetics company. I did enjoy operations, especially traveling to Taiwan and Malaysia putting together the packaging of the Laura Mercier products as they were developed. And it was fun having Karleen and the kids working in the warehouse—picking, packing, and shipping the product. The little warehouse we rented for that part of the business became our family office for the first year, and it was quite fun. My mother even came to help us in the warehouse on occasion, so it was a multigenerational workforce for a short period of time. What could go wrong?

My First of What Would Be an Epic String of Mistakes

DURING THE LAST FEW YEARS at Babbage's, for the first time in my life I had real value in my stockholdings. I decided to leave 100 percent of my Babbage's stock ownership in the new NeoStar Retail Group, as I believed it would go to the moon in the coming years.

Sadly, I had begun to believe my own press clippings, a dumb thing for me to do and further proof I had not gained the personal experience, business maturity, and financial acumen I thought I had. Karleen and I had gone out and bought a great home in 1993 that was likely more than we should have afforded. We got the maximum mortgage we could and still needed a loan for the balance, as we were short of funds. I went to Bank One, where I had my banking relationship, and they were happy to give us a margin loan for that amount. When I took the new $3 million margin loan to start Laura Mercier, Bank One simply added that $3 million to my margin account, which meant that I had now pledged my Babbage's stock as collateral for two loans: one for a new house a couple of years earlier and now this loan to start our cosmetics company. The downside of a margin call was that if the stock price of the collateral sunk to a certain price, the bank could just take the stock, sell it, and pay down the debt. That way they wouldn't have any risk that a loan wouldn't be repaid. That seemed OK, as the Babbage's stock price would have to drop below four dollars a share before I might have a margin call, and the lowest it had been since our IPO was ten dollars a share, while it had been as high as thirty dollars a share. I felt OK with coverage of stock to the loan size, but between my home loan and the seed capital I was providing for Laura Mercier, I did have a slug of my Babbage's stock tied up as collateral. I knew that was risky, but I was so certain that Laura Mercier would be a hit that I didn't really care. And I was so strong in my belief that Babbage's—or whatever the newly combined companies would be called—would continue to grow and prosper.

Panic in the Austin Airport

IN OCTOBER OF 1996, I had just left an Electronic Arts board meeting in Austin and arrived at the Austin airport to await my flight back to Dallas. While I was sitting in the waiting area at the Southwest Airlines gate, I saw a *Wall Street Journal*, picked it up, and started reading to kill time until my flight boarded. As I turned to the stock pages, I checked the EA stock price and then distinctly remember wondering how Babbage's stock was doing. I knew they had changed names to NeoStar Retail Group and looked for the symbol. When I saw a price of around $1.50, I did a double take. That couldn't be right. Did I have the right symbol? What had happened? As I stared at the page, everything began slowing down like I was paralyzed. My mind was whirling—if the stock price was that low, why hadn't I gotten a margin call? Why wasn't Bank One all over me? What was I going to do? At $1.50 stock price, the total value of all of my Babbage's stock was now less than the amount of the loan I owed. I remember getting up and walking into the Austin airport bathroom and throwing up. I was beside myself. I had gone broke! I had four kids in private schools, a multimillion-dollar home, and was being counted on to continue financing Laura Mercier Cosmetics, which had incidentally run through its cash. I was planning to borrow more money on margin to keep Laura Mercier afloat. I sat back down in the chair in the waiting area, and so many thoughts were going through my head. At some point I looked up and realized my flight back to Dallas had boarded and left without me. I had actually sat in the waiting area so numb about what to do that I completely missed my flight. By a lot!

I decided I needed to do two things immediately. First, I needed to call Ron Steinhart, the president of Bank One, and let him know that I had busted a covenant of my margin loan. I couldn't keep it from him, as it had been my commitment when I took the loan. And I needed to immediately contact Bill Morgan, my terrific tax accountant, and ask him what in the heck to do. That was my plan—past that I had no idea. I was taking out virtually no salary from Laura Mercier, so I was in double trouble and knew I had to act fast. My first call was to Ron Steinhart. Ron told me he was available, so I scheduled the meeting. Then I scheduled a meeting with Bill Morgan. I was totally embarrassed and wanted to at least have a game plan. My meeting with Ron went much better than I could have imagined. He had assembled a group of people in his conference, and we sat down. I told the room exactly what had happened at the Austin airport and that I determined I must come clean with Bank One ASAP and work out a plan to move forward in light of my busted covenant. After some questions, Ron said something like, "Gary, none of us can remember a bank customer ever coming in here to tell us they had busted a covenant. Frankly, none of us knew about Babbage's problems either. That is our fault. But you were honest, and we appreciate that. You tell us how much time you think you need to get the money to make this all right." I said that it likely could take me twelve months. Ron told me and the room that in light of my honesty, they would give me a full twelve months to pay back what was owed. I thanked them all and left, noting the power of open and honest communications in business relationships.

My meeting with Bill Morgan was what I needed. No one knew my personal finances better than Bill. Bill was from a small town in West Texas and had a personality such that when he would start scratching his head, Columbo style, and asking lots of questions, you could count on him to be about to say something so smart it would surprise everyone in the room. I laid it all out for Bill, and sure enough, scratching his head and asking questions, he cut right to the chase. He said, "Gary, you have three assets you can sell to generate cash to pay back the bank. First, you can sell Laura Mercier. Second, you can sell your house; and third, you are your own best asset. You aren't taking much money out of Laura Mercier. I understand why, but you now need a real job that will pay you a fair salary for what value you create and contribute. In other words, you can no longer work at Laura Mercier for so little pay. And I believe you must succeed with at least two of these three in order to pull yourself out of this mess over the next twelve months." That was exactly what I needed to hear. Have a plan and then move heaven and earth to make it happen. I had to monetize two of my three biggest assets very quickly to get out of the hole. I could feel the load lifting from my shoulders. I could do this . . .

The Triple Lindy: Selling Laura Mercier

IT WAS A HUGE RELIEF for me to know that I had to sell my stake in Laura Mercier. I owned two-thirds of the company and had become unhappy with it. I had always heard that cosmetics was a tough industry, and when I had overseen the cosmetics division at Sanger-Harris, I had seen that firsthand. But I had not been on the vendor side of the table until Laura Mercier. It was very rough and tumble. Being rude to others seemed to be acceptable behavior. People said anything at any given time to get whatever was wanted, truth be damned, and everything was always a negotiation. For the first time in my career, I began wondering about the notion of respect for others. At the time, I had thought it was axiomatic, especially due to the success we had at Babbage's. But obviously it wasn't. I saw team members leaving the office some days almost slumped over. I checked in with team members from time to time, but especially when they looked beaten down. And indeed, many were. Respect for others was missing from a lot of the company, and the personalities were such that I knew I couldn't legislate good behavior with any hope of success.

While three Laura Mercier team members in particular, Sharon
Collier, Diane Laner, and Bob Hurtte, were terrific, extremely tal-
ented, and very respectful people who provided the much-needed glue
holding the company together, it didn't feel like a company where my
particular skills would be effective over the long term. I now had my
excuse, or, should I say, good reason but just not the real reason, for
selling the company.

Janet was well suited for the kind of work she was doing. I told
her the truth about why I was going to sell my part of the company
and exit, and she completely understood. I believe she was actually
a bit happy to hear it. She had gotten her entrepreneurial legs under
her and was enjoying her notoriety as an entrepreneurial cofounder. If
I could gracefully exit and be replaced by a more corporate entity to
oversee the company, she could perhaps further learn and grow in her
entrepreneurial role.

The timing for my attempt to sell Laura Mercier was fortuitous.
Neiman Marcus had embarked on a strategic initiative to buy select
suppliers in order to better control distribution at the high end of the
market. We seemed to have the profile that fit their new strategy. With
Janet having been a senior officer at Neiman Marcus, our availability to
be acquired moved straight to the top of the acquisition opportunities
for the owner of Neiman Marcus, a Boston-based company named
General Cinema. As I thought about how to price the company, I had
learned enough to know that when you are a young company without
earnings yet, you can often command a higher valuation than if you did
indeed have earnings. While that sounds crazy, and I don't disagree,
for a company with earnings there are all sorts of ways to properly
value the company, especially using a multiple of earnings or earnings
before interest, taxes, depreciation, and amortization (EBITDA). For
a company with losses but with bright prospects, it is easier to value the
company based off of projected revenues. And, of course, we were very
optimistic, having earned our way into all the Neiman Marcus stores,

including Bergdorf Goodman in New York City. We were also in an array of specialty stores in the United States and Europe and thinking of moving into Asia. We were unprofitable still, but we had a great and bright future with lots of future revenues and projected earnings that we could use to price our company.

All I remember of that era was that it took General Cinema almost the entire year I had been given to get to a deal to give us a $12 million valuation, which was 1.5 times our revenues at the time. During the time General Cinema was negotiating to buy Laura Mercier, because I was on the ropes financially, I had raised second round funds to keep Laura Mercier afloat from friends and family by promising them all a minimum 20 percent return on their investment. My two-thirds of the General Cinema valuation cleared my debt at Bank One and allowed me to pay back my friends and family, giving each of them a 20 percent return. It was a nice start on fixing my problems, but after taxes it didn't really put much cash in my pocket.

The Triple Lindy: Selling the House

ONCE AGAIN, WE WERE ABLE to use a good reason for selling the house instead of a real reason! I was too embarrassed to tell anyone I was forty-six years old, a successful entrepreneur, and close to going broke. And besides, it was none of anyone's business. Our kids gave us the good reason to sell our house, which sure sounded like a real reason, and perhaps would have been in normal times, but I wasn't living in normal times. Long story short, there had been a few "unauthorized" parties, which could have been the real reason we sold our house, so we put our house on the market and sold it relatively quickly at full price.

The Triple Lindy: Getting a Paying Job

WHILE BILL MORGAN SAID ALL I needed to do was to succeed with two of the three objectives, I pushed for a trifecta. I was very angry at myself for putting my family in such financial jeopardy, so I wanted to sell the house, sell Laura Mercier, *and* get a real job that I liked, working with people I respected and liked for real compensation. As it happened, my next gig was completely unpredicted and under serendipitous circumstances. Yet it turned into something fun and lucrative over the following few years, and it provided me yet more experiences that helped me toward setting in place my own Leadership Principles. During this time period, when the Laura Mercier sale was near closing, I got a call from a recruiter I knew asking if I would be interested in a board position. I said yes, and we discussed two opportunities he was working, both in the junior apparel sectors. I had great background for those opportunities from my early department-store days. And I was still pretty current on teen trends since I had two teenage daughters at home. We agreed that the recruiter would show me two similar opportunities, but I could only select one, as the two companies competed on some levels. I agreed. One of the firms was a junior swimwear retailer based in Dallas—I can't remember the name, but it was large and growing, with a good reputation. The other was a company called Hot Topic: a goth junior sportswear chain based in Southern California. After meeting with both companies, I simply couldn't see myself joining either board. I surprised myself by deciding during the interview process that I didn't really want back into that world, and I think I was underwhelmed with the people I met at each concept. I told the recruiter no to both of the opportunities.

I assumed that would be the last I would ever hear from the recruiter, but within weeks I was back on a call from him. He told me that I owed him one and that he wanted me to fly to Washington, DC, to meet a man named Tom Carr. Tom was the CEO of CarrAmerica, a large commercial real estate investment trust (REIT) based in DC that had been in business in the DC area since the late 1800s. Tom wanted to discuss the CarrAmerica investment in the serviced-office business with me. At the time I couldn't spell serviced offices, much less spell REIT, but I quickly learned as I got to know Tom.

I learned that the serviced-office business is really simple. You lease an entire floor of a building, and since you were leasing such a large space, your rent rate was really low. You then chop that floor into many small offices and lease them one at a time for a much higher price than you paid for leasing the entire floor. I learned there is a universe of small businesses and professions in which the owner or executive works alone. They typically look for office space that impresses visitors when they walk onto the floor—it looks like the entire floor is their workplace, which is the object of that concept. There are additional services and amenities, like a receptionist sitting at the entrance to announce all visitors, break rooms, conference rooms, and other amenities that a small company couldn't afford on its own. The serviced-office sector was highly fragmented, and the real estate market was ripe for a roll-up of such a fragmented market located in their office buildings. Tom offered me a job at very high pay to help him roll up that sector in the United States and in Europe.

The actual serviced-office company CarrAmerica owned was based in Atlanta, Georgia, and was named OmniOffices. I had to commute to Atlanta every week, which I viewed as a kind of penance for having screwed up my family finances. I would fly into Atlanta on Sunday night or early Monday morning and return to Dallas on Thursday evenings. We had offices around the country, so it was easy for me to work a couple of days early in any week in Atlanta and then visit other OmniOffice locations for a couple of days and then get back to Dallas, where there were also OmniOffice locations where I could hang my hat on Fridays.

OmniOffices had been started by a very eccentric person, which I learned was pretty much how the entire industry was built—by crazy entrepreneurs! I was happy as I could be because I could be accused of being a crazy entrepreneur myself. I was also lucky enough to meet Joe Wallace, who was Tom's right-hand person in the company and was the person who knew the most about the serviced-office business. We hit it off famously, and the game was on. With their budding superstar sales leader Jennifer Goodwyn growing and learning by the day, we were in a great position to dominate.

Within about twelve months, not only had we rolled up a lot of additional locations but so had a competitor, Vantas. We had become the two biggest serviced-office companies in the United States. Vantas made CarrAmerica an offer they couldn't refuse for OmniOffices, with the only stipulation being that the OmniOffices executive team be the team to run the newly combined entity. Were it not for Joe and Jennifer, I doubt I would have stayed, but I had been around the block enough times to know the value of world-class team members, and Joe and Jennifer were two for sure. In addition, there was just a terrific amount of talent throughout the OmniOffices team that had me excited about our future. Tom had cut me a good deal, not just on cash compensation, but also with ownership equity in OmniOffices when I joined the company. When Tom and I discussed the Vantas offer we received to sell OmniOffices, and the fact that I would have a new chairman overseeing me, he also told me what the combination would be worth to me personally with my equity stake. It was dramatically beyond my expectations! It took care of all my financial issues, and I realized for the first time that I had some real money. I paid off all my debts, renovated the new home we had just bought with proceeds from the sales of the other home, and still had a nice nest egg to put away for Karleen and me.

I had hit my trifecta. I had sold Laura Mercier Cosmetics, I had sold our home, and now I had a great job—one that in addition to paying me a really nice salary and bonus opportunity had already given me enough equity that I made more money than I had from selling Babbage's stock in the years before its bankruptcy. I decided to let a money manager manage our newly found nest egg so I could focus on work. I'm not sure how we landed at Deutsche Bank's private wealth management group, but we did. We must have been referred by someone who had a bone to pick with me! Without even meeting other money managers, we signed up with Deutsche Bank. What a monster mistake that was!

The Tax Shelter
Gone Wrong

WE HAD A LOT OF money from the OmniOffices sale and wanted the team at Deutsche Bank to present us with an investment plan to go forward. Before long they presented what they felt was a fail-safe plan to shelter 100 percent of my gain from the sale of OmniOffices. We had a meeting in their offices, and joining them were representatives from KPMG, a major accounting firm in America at that time, and also lawyers from Jenkens & Gilchrist, a nationally famous white-shoe law firm that had been started in Dallas. They all assured us that the tax shelter they were proposing we use to offset our gain was 100 percent within the law and that it just took advantage of some tax loopholes. The law firm said they would give us a "comfort letter," which is legalese for a letter from the law firm saying they had looked at the shelter and that it was legal. The accounting firm offered the same kind of letter about the accounting to make the shelter work. And Deutsche Bank wealth managers in the meeting stated that their global firm stood behind this shelter. I told them I wanted my own advisers to weigh in, and we agreed to a follow-up meeting.

I decided Karleen and I should have both Bill Morgan and Jill Louis, a lawyer I had met when she worked as an attorney helping us start Laura Mercier, review the plan. Bill and Jill agreed to meet Karleen and me at the Deutsche Bank offices to hear the pitch. After hearing the pitch, they each gave me their gut reactions. Bill was a veteran tax accountant and tax attorney and told me that though the tax shelter they were proposing might be legitimate and within the letter of the law, it didn't feel like it was within the spirit of the law. Jill, a recent graduate of Harvard Law School, told me that she remembered her tax professor hammering on the class that the tax laws were a mess, and if there were found loopholes in the law, they should be taken advantage of as long as the loopholes were legal. While Jill didn't have advice past that, she felt that Bill had probably said it best. The tax shelter was perhaps within the letter of the law but not within the spirit of the tax law. And with that advice, I made a decision to go along with the shelter since it would save me a significant tax bill. I also let Bill and Jill know that if the IRS even brought it up as an issue, much less vomited on it, I would immediately pay back all taxes with interest and any penalties if required to just move past it.

Long story short, it *did* blow up, and almost by return mail I paid all back taxes with interest. I was able to get out of that disaster very quickly and painlessly, but for many other investors, it was ugly! Jill Louis and I remain dear friends; she is the managing partner of the Dallas office of Perkins Coie, and I would never make a move in business without checking in with Jill first. Over time, we moved our investment management from Deutsche Bank to Kerry Wildenthal at UBS and have been clients of Kerry's for over twenty-five years. Kerry has become so essential to all of us in the family and feels like an extended family member herself! Karleen and I have watched both Jill and Kerry grow their families and careers, and they have watched our family do the same. They are not only incredibly capable at what they do, they are both world-class human beings!

HQ Global Workplaces

I DID NOT GET ALONG very well with the new owner of OmniOffices, which is sad since I had so thoroughly enjoyed my work with Tom Carr. While the new chairman of the combined companies was also a next-generation real estate guy in a long-standing family real estate business, just like Tom Carr, I felt he was brash and arrogant. He was deferential to me generally; however, I certainly wasn't on any sort of regular meeting schedule with him, which suited me just fine. Our first order of business, exactly like when Babbage's and Software Etc. completed the combination of equals, was to find a new name for the combined company. I'm not sure I remember the process we used to arrive at HQ Global Workplaces. We may have used a branding firm, or possibly our new owner told us what he wanted the new name to be. In any case, we moved forward.

Vantas was based in New York City, and OmniOffices was based in Atlanta. I felt that we needed a new combined company headquarters location so we could build a new team that was up to the task of running what was now one of the three largest serviced-office companies in the world. With no pushback from my boss, I moved the company to Dallas. That obviously allowed me to be home, but as a result I also created a new executive group on top of the New York team and the Atlanta team. The sales teams all remained in the field, with each group keeping their own accounting teams to start.

There were now three major global competitors in the space. The other two were Servcorp and Regus. I probably met with Servcorp at least five times, and with Regus at least that many times also. Both companies took the bait on wanting a business combination. With permission from my boss, I began talks with each about what a business combination might look like.

These two stops along my journey, Laura Mercier and HQ Global Workplaces, were important for me, if for no other reason than that I now had firm comparisons between Babbage's and other businesses. Not surprisingly, observing the differences in culture between these companies and what I had spent twelve years developing at Babbage's was very instructive for me. At HQ, the first half of the assignment was a real joy for me. Tom Carr, the owner of OmniOffices, was an exceptional leader, and I was very comfortable with him. The OmniOffices team was similarly impressive, with super leaders throughout the company, some of whom I hired later while I was at Kinko's. They were just superb businesspeople, this in spite of hearing that a prior owner sometimes threw telephones against the wall!

It was starting to occur to me more starkly that it was OK for me to arrive at some leadership principles simply by watching the negative impact of a lack of a codified guiding principle. For instance, in twelve years at Babbage's and in six years in department stores, while I clearly had seen isolated instances of bad behavior, I had not seen ongoing examples of lack of respect from leadership until after my time at Babbage's.

It's one thing to want to codify the notion of continuous improvement inside a company. That's easy to do and very acceptable to team members, as it is a noble ideal in any company. Respect for others, honesty, and integrity rise to a level of importance that, as obvious as it may seem to some, become necessary because of the toxicity that can develop if they are not specifically laid out as guiding principles for a highly functioning culture.

Key Lessons

PART 5

Stay Ahead of Change:

Success can breed complacency. Always challenge the status quo, even when business is booming. Continuous improvement isn't a catchphrase—it's a survival strategy.

The Power of Honesty:

Transparency isn't just about avoiding trouble; it's about building trust. When faced with financial challenges, being up-front can save you from disaster.

Acknowledge Your Missteps:

Own your mistakes. It's the only way to learn from them. Never allow ego to blind you to the reality of your situation.

Embrace Every Opportunity:

When the path you're on starts to close, look for doors that are opening elsewhere. Transition can lead to transformation.

Maximize Your Assets:

Understand what you have and how to leverage it. Sometimes the most significant asset you have is your own experience and expertise.

Strategic Partnerships Matter:
Whether it's cofounding a company or merging giants, the right partnerships can amplify your capabilities and create new opportunities.

Respect Is Non-negotiable:
A culture without respect is unsustainable. Ensure that your environment upholds the dignity of every team member.

Negotiate with Integrity:
In business dealings, keep your word and expect others to do the same. A deal is not just about the numbers; it's about the people and promises behind them.

Seek Varied Perspectives:
In moments of uncertainty, consult with trusted advisors. A diverse set of eyes can offer new insights and solutions.

Acknowledge the Personal Impact of Business Decisions:
Business isn't just business—it's personal. The choices you make can affect lives, careers, and relationships. Handle them with care.

Recognize When to Let Go:
Not all ventures are meant for eternity. Knowing when to exit is as crucial as knowing when to enter.

Principles Over Profit:
If a deal or strategy feels like it's skirting the edge of your ethical boundaries, it's OK to walk away. Your principles are the bedrock of your reputation and legacy.

Diversify Your Dependence:
Relying on a single source of success is risky. Spread your bets to ensure one setback doesn't capsize your entire ship.

PART SIX

WEAVING LEADERSHIP PRINCIPLES INTO THE WORKPLACE

My Career To Date Had Been the Dress Rehearsal for Kinko's

I BEGAN SPENDING MORE TIME with Dan Connors during my HQ Global Workplaces assignment. Dan was a Bain team member who was doing work for us at HQ. Dan looked like he was out of central casting for his Bain role. He was conservative in his dress—with his khakis and button-down shirts well starched and a trim haircut. The only thing sharper than his intellect was his bedside manner. He could dumb down concepts so well that even I could understand them. And he never got frustrated when he had to flesh things out for anyone who missed the point. It really was Dan's superpower. We both really liked each other, and during one conversation he let me know that Bain had a process for Bain employees to jump to clients of Bain and become employed by that client. This was a seismic shift from eighteen years earlier, when Bill Bain threatened to sue Jim for trying to leave the company to start Babbage's with me. Dan was obviously letting me know that he would be interested in joining the HQ team if there was room for him. I took this opportunity to tell him that I was likely going to find a way out of HQ, hopefully through a sale to Regus or Servcorp, but in any case, there was a limit to how much time I would spend there with my current boss. With all that knowledge, Dan remained undeterred, and we started the process that led to him jumping over to HQ from Bain. It also would end up being the key to my success at Kinko's. Dan was and remains an extraordinary executive and—leaving aside his poor judgment in wanting to ride my coattails, short as they were—I felt extremely lucky to have him join the team.

My tip about the job search commencing for a new CEO at Kinko's came from my sister Melanie. She has been a high performer her entire career and has been vice chair of two of the largest recruiting firms in the world for almost twenty years: Heidrick & Struggles for the first five years and then Korn Ferry for almost fifteen years. Melanie has always been a big cheerleader for whatever I was doing, which is pretty cool because she has also always been my personal claim to fame. While Melanie has never told me which clients she is working for currently or what positions she is trying to fill, and she could never submit my name in a search, as it was against all rules of recruiting, it was less of a problem to make me aware of job openings in the market, so long as she or her firm weren't involved. And from time to time over her career she has done that. She saved her best for last. One day in late 2000, she let me know that Clayton, Dubilier & Rice, a large private equity firm in New York City that owned Kinko's, was going to start a search for a new Kinko's CEO. Apparently, Kinko's was doing very poorly, and they needed a new CEO to turn it around. That was my lead of a lifetime—and my ticket out of a situation where I knew I couldn't stay much longer. And all of this was happening on a timeline that matched Dan Connors joining me at HQ Global Workplaces as EVP and head of strategy.

I filled Dan in on the opportunity, and he lit up—this could also be his lottery ticket if he joined me at Kinko's and we were smart enough to pull this off. Dan started learning everything he could about Kinko's and thinking about what a turnaround plan might involve. I immediately started to visit Kinko's stores all over Dallas. And I read everything I could get my hands on, not just about Kinko's but also about Clayton, Dubilier & Rice. While I was doing that, I was also pushing conversations about Regus potentially buying HQ Global Workplaces. And I had never had so much fun and been as energized about anything as I was about this. If you think about it, we were facing yet another business Triple Lindy!

1. Figure out how to get Regus to buy HQ Global Workplaces.
2. Figure out how to get myself named CEO of Kinko's.
3. If we successfully completed steps one and two, then figure out how to turn around Kinko's, which was in very bad shape!

It was actually more challenging than that, as it all had to be sequential. I stood to make a lot of money if we could sell HQ to Regus, which was the global consolidation the industry really needed. It didn't matter if HQ bought Regus or vice versa; the consolidation would help both companies immensely. And in the scenario that Regus bought HQ, that consolidation would trigger my employment contract, which stipulated that in a sale with change of control going to a buyer, I would get a payout of my contract. In either scenario I would win. Even if I didn't have the Kinko's opportunity, Regus buying HQ would have triggered my contract. Combine that with the fact that the HQ chairman also very badly wanted Regus to acquire HQ, it was a perfect situation for me.

I also didn't want to jeopardize my Kinko's opportunity by dragging my feet with the Regus combination or getting caught during this potential jump to the next rock in my career. The owner of HQ was a pretty volatile guy who had an ego that required he be the smartest person in the room. If he caught on to my Kinko's prospect, there would be no telling what he might do. I had to keep him focused with me on getting the Regus deal done as a first order. We both began working our networks to make HQ a target for Regus, and then I planned to dangle Regus's interest in HQ to Servcorp to see if we could make the sale an auction!

Catching the Eye of CD&R

THE SECOND ORDER OF BUSINESS was catching the attention of Clayton, Dubilier & Rice. Typically, that would go through the recruiter, and in this case the recruiter who had won the Kinko's search, Jim Citrin, was head of the CEO practice at Spencer Stuart, a top-tier recruiting firm. He and my sister frequently competed for the same sorts of engagements, so there wasn't much love lost between them. I decided I wouldn't have appeared on any list of candidates that Jim Citrin might be submitting to the CD&R team. I dug around until I found that George Tamke, a partner at CD&R, was the partner in charge of the Kinko's investment. A little further digging revealed that George had been a very successful business executive in his career, including serving as CEO of Emerson Electric, before going to CD&R as an operating partner. CD&R was organized quite differently from most private equity firms at that time. For virtually all PE firms, the financial partners were "the tip of the spear." Finance partners sourced firms, cut the deals, created the board of directors and the investment thesis, before meeting regularly with their portfolio companies to measure success. CD&R was completely different. Their "tips of the spear" were their operating partners, and they had an impressive list of operating partners, including many partners with George Tamke's level of background success in corporate America. For example, Jack Welch was an operating partner at CD&R after he left his role as CEO of General Electric.

I decided to cold-call George, and he took my call. I introduced myself and told him I should be a candidate for the job. I discussed my background, and he agreed. He told me that Jim Citrin was running the placement for CD&R, and I told him I knew and gave him the background on why I was calling him directly. Apparently, my sister had pitched the placement also, and Citrin had won the search contract for CD&R. I told George playfully that I was glad Jim Citrin won or the perfect candidate for the job would never have been introduced to him. George laughed and said he would speak with Jim Citrin and would make sure I was interviewed.

Bottom line, I flew through the interview process and made it to the final two candidates. They did the deepest background search I had ever experienced, including finding out how many traffic tickets I'd had (too many!). But, finally, I made it to a board dinner in St. Louis, where I was interviewed by several individuals and then the entire group from CD&R. I felt very good, and George told me that they had to meet the other candidate, so it might be a couple of weeks before he could get back to me. There were enough nods and winks that I felt very sure I was going to be offered the job.

Why Such Confidence in My Ability to Impact Kinko's?

HERE IS WHY I FELT so positive about my ability to create value at Kinko's. I had read everything I could about the history of Kinko's and its founder, Paul Orfalea. Paul was unique. He had severe dyslexia and ADHD while growing up. He couldn't hold down a job and needed substantial help just getting through school. But he had entrepreneurial blood coursing through his veins, and in visits to colleges, he saw students lining up for copy machines. They needed copiers for much of their coursework, and it was incredibly tough for students in the early 1970s to find copiers to use that were affordable and available whenever and wherever they were needed. Orfalea saw that problem and put together a solution across the street from the University of California, Santa Barbara. It was an immediate hit. Kinko's grew across America by moving to university town after university town and winning all the university student business. They then began expansion into nonuniversity communities. When college students who spent their university years using Kinko's began moving to other cities to start their careers, they continued using Kinko's. It became part of the fabric of their lives.

Paul was a big believer in giving team members "a fraction of the action," both those on the floor of their stores and the partners who signed on for each major market in the United States. By the mid-1990s, most major markets in America had Kinko's, with over 120 partners owning all the one thousand plus locations. It was a dream for the private equity world, as they knew that professionalizing the systems and processes across an incredibly fragmented network would produce fabulous results. They were quite correct, but also very wrong.

There are basically two ways to run businesses. One way is called "command and control." Think the military, where the generals figure out what to do and tell their people what they want done, and the people who report to them figure out how to make what the generals want happen. The military is very, very systematic, and everyone knows the rules. You salute your commanding officer and say "yes, sir" or "no, sir," salute again, and then go about your business of doing exactly what you were told. Everything is a command from the top down, and everything works because everyone is controlled. Big companies mostly run like that too. If you look at any of the historically best-managed companies in America, you will find mostly command-and-control managers overseeing the entire corporate environments. From General Electric to IBM to J.P. Morgan bank and FedEx, each is run by a CEO who rules with an iron fist. No one bucks the reporting lines of authority.

And then there is the other way to run a business. Some companies are founded by entrepreneurs who think very differently and believe that decision-making is best when distributed to the people who live with the results of the decisions. There is usually more worker-friendly compensation relative to profit sharing and a general belief that team members are better off asking for forgiveness than permission. It is the entrepreneurial way.

I am an advocate of the entrepreneurial approach, though I absolutely believe that command and control has its place, particularly in very large companies where all the processes must be the same across the entire company in order for the company to operate most efficiently. A great example of command-and-control management is FedEx, where I had the incredible privilege of being the ninth member of the FedEx Strategic Management Committee (SMC). The SMC was the committee that oversaw FedEx globally. It met every Friday without fail at 8:00 a.m. in Memphis, with Fred Smith, the direct supervisor of every member of the SMC, presiding. Reporting directly to Fred Smith from 2004 to 2006 was the greatest privilege of my working career. Fred was an iconic entrepreneur, who came up with his idea for FedEx in college and wrote an essay on why it was a great idea. He got a C on that paper! And when he almost ran out of cash to make payroll at the start of FedEx, he went to Las Vegas to make enough money gambling to meet payroll. He was a classic entrepreneur, but he was also ex-military, which means he understood command and control completely. And as FedEx grew into a global behemoth with 275,000 employees during my tenure, Fred had morphed his company into a command-and-control-style company with him making all strategic decisions. FedEx could turn on a dime because if Fred declared that next Tuesday morning at 2:00 a.m. the entire FedEx organization would strategically veer two degrees to starboard, at 2:00 a.m. the company would veer exactly as they were told.

As I think about it, maybe the fact that Fred started as an entrepreneur is why I liked him so much and vice versa. My time with Fred really was magical, and I'll get to that, but now, back to Kinko's founder Paul Orfalea.

Paul was a classic entrepreneur, and the Clayton, Dubilier & Rice operating partners were by definition command and control. That was the fatal flaw in CD&R's initial strategy to combine the 120 plus partnerships existing at Kinko's into one platform and then roll up into a larger, more profitable company. The first CEO they recruited for Kinko's was a classic command-and-control manager. Joe Hardin had been CEO of Sam's Club and had been very successful in his role there. He was a great candidate for Kinko's CEO, or so CD&R thought. Because CD&R partners didn't understand the amount of entrepreneurial DNA that existed inside Kinko's, they couldn't have forecast what would happen when a strong command-and-control CEO began attempting to force his will onto not just a group of owners who controlled each of their 120 partnerships as individual fiefdoms, but also all the way down to the shop floor.

It started with Joe trying to bring consistency to Kinko's. He started laying out directives for consistent store sizes, consistent color schemes, consistent pricing, consistent bidding on jobs, consistent staffing norms, and more. These all made sense on some level, especially if you were oriented toward command and control. But to a company partnership that thrived on independence, this felt like the government encroaching on their liberties. As a result, passive-aggressive behaviors ensued. While CD&R had paid every Kinko's partner for their equity in Kinko's, it kept each of them in their home area and called them district managers. This helped develop an organization hierarchy that reflected most one-thousand-store chains in America. But these past owners, now called district managers, dealt with Joe in the following way when he would travel to their markets. They first tried smiling and suggesting that whatever Joe asked them to do had been tried before in their "district" and didn't work. When Joe politely told them to try again and to please do it his way, they said they certainly would. That was obviously the response Joe would have gotten at Sam's Club. Joe would then jump on a plane and head to the next market. As soon as he left town, the district manager, who had been the founder and partner in charge of the market for many years, would tell all of the team members to disregard what Joe had said and to go about business as usual. The team members did that with the approval and admiration of Paul Orfalea, who truly despised the CD&R team. That feeling was mutual. I began describing Kinko's to CD&R as "the people's republic of Kinko's." It would get a round of laughter but also imparted to CD&R a better understanding of what the situation was and what needed to happen to correct it.

Ultimately, when performance dropped to a level that suggested that Kinko's could die an untimely death and losses would keep mounting, they fired Joe and set about finding an entrepreneur who could appeal to the hearts and minds of Kinko's team members while still being able to make necessary changes to the way Kinko's did business.

I was a pretty logical candidate. I had been involved with a company that had grown from one to hundreds of locations and from a hierarchy that was highly entrepreneurial to one that had set standards for doing business. I had successfully started but also sold Laura Mercier Cosmetics, demonstrating that I knew how to sell a company. The icing on the cake for CD&R was my serviced-office stint, where I rolled up many smaller businesses into one large company, followed by selling that company to another larger company. They were fairly convinced that I could potentially turn Kinko's around. And I had a secret weapon they didn't even know about: Dan Connors.

The Deal and the HQ Exit

I ULTIMATELY WAS OFFERED the CEO job at Kinko's and spent a good amount of time negotiating my contract. Along with the financial considerations, I asked for time to resolve the potential sale of HQ to Regus, one way or the other. The CD&R partners were sympathetic to my desire to make another score on the sale of HQ, so they gave me a period of time to get that done. And it was during this time that Dan worked almost full time developing a hundred-day plan for us when we stepped into Kinko's. Dan knew (as did the partners from CD&R) that I was going to name him EVP and head of strategy and business development on day one, minute one. He was all in and as excited as I was. We were having some serious fun! And since we were playing with house money, meaning that we didn't really have to sell HQ to jump to Kinko's, we were working hard to sell HQ but in a pretty stress-free way. We hoped we could sell it, as that was the outcome both we and the HQ chairman wanted. But if it didn't work out, we still had an enormous opportunity at Kinko's. It took a long time to develop our hundred-day plan, but it was professionally assembled, properly tipping its hat to the power of the entrepreneur-based Kinko's culture. It perfectly set the table for turning Kinko's around, and we began itching to get out of HQ.

My contract with HQ was clear that if I were fired without cause, I would get one year of salary as severance. That means that if I was fired just because my boss thought I was doing a bad job, I would still get one year of salary. And that was a bunch of money! I met with an employment-law attorney and learned what I could do to make it a firing without cause. I made my move. I set a meeting with my boss and sat in front of him and told him he must be disappointed in me for not being able to pull off the Regus combination. He agreed that he was. I was just speaking the truth to him. I suggested that knowing he hadn't felt like I worked as well with him as others might, I understood that he might be thinking about firing me. He got very cautious at that point and shut down. I told him to think about it, but I would certainly understand if he wanted to fire me.

As I figured out by his response, he had thought I might have another deal put together, and he handed me a severance agreement with several pages of companies that I could not jump into and still qualify for twelve months of HQ salary since each listed company was competitive in his mind. The company list he handed me looked like he had boiled the ocean and come up with almost every name of every retailer in America and virtually all the real estate firms also! He had a very smug attitude, figuring that he had me where he wanted—he could fire me and not have to pay me any severance. After again checking with my attorney, I signed the severance agreement with no changes, which made my boss cringe, as he figured out that I must be jumping to somewhere he didn't know. He was correct, and I had coordinated with CD&R and the Kinko's PR person and had the press release ready to go. The very next day after the ink dried on the HQ severance agreement, Kinko's dropped the press release. My boss went nuts. His lawyers contacted my lawyer, but we ultimately won the day. For the next twelve months I was paid twice: by Kinko's *and* by HQ. While it wasn't close to the money I would have made if the deal had been consummated (which it was a couple of years later), it was oh, so gratifying! Looking back on this chapter of my career, it feels, and indeed was, very petty. But it felt good: this person was such an expert at pushing people around and had been such a thorn in my side culturally when compared to my senior team.

The Laura Mercier and HQ Global Workplaces experiences were kind of the opposite of what the Babbage's experience had been. And as I mentioned earlier, I was realizing that you have to also see bad management environments to be completely sure of what sorts of guiding principles are most aligned with your view of healthy management. You can know what you have liked, but knowing what you *don't* like allows you to have a more nuanced view of what constitutes a healthy corporate culture. I was making real strides toward my set of Leadership Principles!

The Kinko's Turnaround Begins

THE THIRD AND FINAL MOVEMENT in achieving this Triple Lindy was to actually turn Kinko's around. Of course, with Kinko's having lost about $11 million in EBITDA in the twelve months prior to Dan and me arriving in July of 2001, we knew all too well that we would have to hit the ground running. The hundred-day plan had several pillars, but most important was that we had to get out into the network of stores to learn what the people on the front lines of Kinko's thought the company issues were and get their input on what would need to happen for us to return to better results. They had had almost five years of my predecessor, and most were not happy with where the company was financially, as bad performance had impacted the store bonuses. Store compensation packages included what Paul Orfalea had called "a fraction of the action," which was a bonus based on each store's success. A super idea! It got the attention of every store team member, from the store manager to the shortest-tenured employee. But the fact was that they had not gotten large bonuses for years due to falling business profits, and the company collectively was in a very bad mood.

Dan and I believed that the core opportunity was for us to "leverage our scale." We had over twelve hundred stores at that time. Some stores were so close to each other geographically that you could literally stand in front of your store and yell at your counterpart down the street. I believe that in St. Louis there was one five-mile stretch of road with five Kinko's stores. Every single store was open twenty-four hours a day. Every single store had the same huge complement of very expensive copy equipment. Each single store used its own service providers. Many stores bought paper from various suppliers. The list went on and on. There were no best practices. There was really nothing happening that promoted creation of profitability by linking a network of stores to pull in the same direction. Heck, two Kinko's stores a mile apart would literally bid against each other on a big printing opportunity. Think about that for a moment. Bidding against yourself!

I had to start somewhere, and on Friday, July 6, 2001, I started my first day at Kinko's, in its headquarters in Ventura, California. Another benefit of being involved with a private equity firm led by ex-corporate CEOs is that they were used to living wherever they wanted to live, so they didn't worry that I was living in Dallas.

My first day of work was an eye-opener. The biggest surprise for me was that, as I walked through the offices when I arrived, I saw a bunch of people wearing wet suits while sitting at desks. I asked a couple of them what was up with the wet suit, and they each said something like, "Surf's up at noon, and I'll be surfing during my lunch break."

The laid-back atmosphere was palpable. I felt no sense of urgency anywhere, which blew me away, as the company had been hemorrhaging cash. After a couple of days at the corporate offices, I had seen enough. It was early July, and I had my admin tentatively set up a meeting for all forty-two regional and district managers, along with all people in management at director level and up. We further communicated that I was going to travel the United States extensively for most of my available time in the coming couple of months, meeting all district managers and holding town halls in each market before I spent too much time in Ventura or met with all the senior officers. Dan and I had agreed that the best use of my time during the early days would be to spend a month or two mostly traveling into all forty-two regions of the company. Since all stores were open 24-7, I would have to host three separate town halls in each market. And I would do the same thing in all forty-two regions of the United States. I had a lot of work in front of me and hit the ground running hard.

While it wasn't a surprise to me since I had seen it my entire career, the quote attributed to Napoleon, "If you want to know what is going on at the front lines, go look!" always wins the day. As an entrepreneur, I always found that the people closest to the customers were also the people who knew best what did and didn't work at a company. By the time I had held town halls all over America, I knew the answer to what ailed Kinko's. It was Ventura! People at the headquarters somehow thought that the company stores should report to the headquarters instead of exactly vice versa! In my analogy in the town halls, I talked about a solar system where headquarters thought it was the sun with twelve hundred stores rotating as planets around it, instead of a solar system where the stores were the sun and the various work centers at the headquarters rotated around the stores. This was contrary to what Joe had instilled and what the headquarters wanted.

Within one week of being on the job, I sent out a company-wide email stating that from that day forward, we would drop the name Kinko's Corporate Offices. We would instead use the term KFSO, Kinko's Field Support Organization, as it better expressed how the organization would work going forward. Everyone got the message, especially at the old KCO headquarters! They began asking why they hadn't had a town hall meeting in Ventura yet. The good reason was that I was traveling so much in the field—and that is what we said. But the *real* reason was that Dan had been doing a chain-of-command analysis and other sorts of examinations of the corporate offices that led us to ultimately believe that we could facilitate a reduction in workforce of about six hundred of the fifteen hundred people currently employed in Ventura. That would result in a right-sized field support organization.

And that was just a start. Dan and I were quite sure once we started to rationalize the field organization—leverage our scale—that more cuts would be able to come. Our work was happening hard and fast, and the first meeting when the field leadership, KFSO leadership, and Dan and I would all come together for three days for a vision session was set. The meeting would be in Denver, Colorado, and the date for the meeting ended up becoming one that will live forever in infamy in the United States. That date was September 11, 2001.

9/11: The Unbelievable Story of Kinko's Involvement

THE DATE IS BURNED INTO anyone's brain who was alive on that day. And it was no different for us, but on the other hand, it *was* different for us. It started at breakfast that morning. I was sitting at a table with other executives when my son Ben called my cell phone. He told me that a plane had crashed into the World Trade Center. We talked about that for a minute, and I told him a plane had once flown into the Empire State Building during World War II. The call ended, and I told the group what Ben had said and what I had said, and we continued our conversation. A short time later, Ben called me again, this time pretty breathless. He told me another plane had hit the other building and that we were under attack. I hung up, and our table quickly switched to talking about what to do. We broke into groups. We needed TVs put into our big conference room so everyone could watch, and we all decided we needed some more information before making the call to cancel the meeting that we all had been so excited about.

Within an hour, all flights in the United States were canceled and all planes grounded. The monumental nature of this was sinking in for all of us. Around 10:00 a.m. mountain time Paul Rostron, our SVP of people, came and asked me to please step into the hall with him. He reported he had just gotten an emergency call from a store manager in Fort Lauderdale, Florida, who urgently needed to speak with me. I was told that he would only speak to me. I told Paul to get him on the line and use the speaker so we would both be able to hear him. Soon we had the store manager on the line. He reminded me he had met me when I toured his store and in the town hall meeting a few weeks earlier. Then he told me that several weeks ago he had been working the late shift, and four guys had come into the store, needing to make copies of a CD. That was a service Kinko's offered, though as it happened the CD burner in his store was broken. He told Paul and me that the four men appeared very anxious to get copies. Since he had a CD burner at his home, he told them if they wanted to leave the CD with him, he would make copies there when he got off of his shift and have them ready by the next morning. That sounded good to them, so they left the CD and said they would be back the next morning. Later he went home and made the copies on his home computer. He said he didn't think much about it other than it was odd that the CD was a training manual and schematics for American Airlines 757 and 767 aircraft, including seating plans and wiring. Once he watched the television that morning, he knew he had to call me. I asked him where he was, and he said he was in his store. I told him to stay there and not speak to anyone, and we would get back to him quickly.

When he hung up, Paul and I agreed this was big news, and I wondered aloud how I could get in touch with the right person. That's when Paul floored me by saying something like, "Well, I can call Uncle Richard." I asked who Uncle Richard was, and Paul told me that Richard Haver was his wife Cindy's uncle and had been selected by Secretary of Defense Donald Rumsfeld as the special assistant to the secretary of defense for intelligence in June of 2001. Cindy's uncle reported directly to Secretary of Defense Rumsfeld. I don't know how the stars managed to align on that one! I told him to do it, and after fumbling around in his contacts, he got Richard Haver on the line. I spoke with Richard and told him everything we had been told. He wanted to put his boss on the line, and then we were speaking directly to Secretary Rumsfeld, who had a series of very smart questions for us. He asked if the store manager still had the cache in his computer. If he did, then the FBI could see exactly what was copied. He also wanted the store manager's home address so the FBI could get a team to his home quickly. Finally, he asked if we had cameras in our stores. Paul knew all these answers, and that was a good thing, as I knew nothing about anything relative to his questions. The answer was that there were twelve active cameras in every single Kinko's store, and each camera kept thirty days of twenty-four-hour video. He told us to have the store manager go to his home and wait for the men he would send there. The store manager met the agents at his home, and they quickly saw the CDs that had been copied. The FBI team rushed to the store and began poring over videos. They found actual footage of the four men in the store on several occasions, including the day I was there. And, incredibly, in addition to the video footage we captured, we saw these same men all sitting at rental computers in that store, paying for rental time on Kinko's personal computers. What they didn't know, and I didn't know either at the time, was that each Kinko's store had about twelve computer stations where people could come to rent time. And those twelve thousand to fourteen thousand rental computers were connected directly to our Kinko's Network Operations Center in Phoenix, along with all the digital video cameras, cash registers, and printers. And this Network Operations Center also kept thirty days of history for each computer, video camera, cash register, and printer. Not only were we able to get the FBI video of the men at our computers, we could also tell which websites they were accessing and what keystrokes they were taking at each website on each computer. By matching the time on the video cameras with the time on the computers, we could actually see them buying their airline tickets for the September 11 flights in our stores, along with communications among other groups of terrorists. If you ever wondered how in the world the United States had photos so quickly of all the hijackers and their tickets and security footage of them going through airports, it was because Kinko's led them to all that information.

Because we were now in complete cooperation with the FBI, we provided all the copy equipment used by the federal government at Ground Zero for the full duration they needed it. And as many as fifty-five FBI agents worked in various Kinko's stores around America, based on real-time information our Network Operations Center was feeding them. Since we now knew which websites the terrorists accessed, we set our Network Operations Center up so each time those websites were accessed by any rental computer in any Kinko's, we knew instantly which store and which computer was being used and forwarded that information quickly to the FBI. Our involvement resulted in our being listed in the final report of the 9/11 Commission. Though very few people inside of Kinko's actually knew what was happening and the level of help we gave to the FBI, those who worked on this project all felt very patriotic but also a bit flummoxed to learn that all of the hijackers had actually bought their airline tickets from inside Kinko's stores and that they had used Kinko's for meetings and its rental computers as communication tools.

Beyond that, the only recognition we got for our work was a mug from the Department of Justice, given to me along with a handshake and them telling me that I was an honorary US Marshal. That mug still sits on my shelf. I remember teasing the FBI agent who gave it to me, saying I wouldn't look a gift horse in the mouth, but it would have been very cool for the mug to say FBI or even CIA instead. He pretty curtly told me that they don't give out such things.

As an aside, the meeting in Denver was obviously canceled, and everyone worked their own way to their homes. Many had to stay until planes started flying again. Dan and I got a rental car and drove back to Dallas from Denver. We drove through a massive migration of tarantulas across the highway in northeastern New Mexico, which could have been straight out of a Stephen King movie and would normally have been the highlight or lowlight of our trip. But me getting stopped by the police west of Amarillo driving 120 miles an hour in a 70 mile per hour zone was very special. As Dan will attest, the policeman actually let me off! It wasn't me smooth talking the policeman. It was the specter of what a policeman has to do after stopping someone going 120 miles per hour or more, which in the end kept the policeman from arresting me. He told me that it was a lot of paperwork. I would have to go to jail and wouldn't be released until the next day, and he, like us, just wanted to get home to his family since the nation was reeling from September 11. He let me go, and I will never forget the look on Dan's face—both pride and disdain in the same smile. Justice was served fifteen miles farther east when I was stopped again, this time driving something like eighty. And this time I got a ticket.

The Make-or-Break Meeting

DAN AND I BOTH KNEW that our next all-hands meeting, which was moved to early November, was going to be critical. We were going to make the case to a) take almost 75 percent of our stores down to twelve- to eighteen-hour days from twenty-four hours, b) consolidate most of the big equipment out of every location and into production centers in each market so every store didn't need so much expensive equipment, and c) which we knew would be incendiary, group store-performance analysis differently to batch stores with similar customer profiles together regardless of geographic location so we could find the best ways to view each store's performance in a particular cohort. For instance, in Chicago there is a store in Wrigleyville, a small suburb near downtown. Of over twelve hundred Kinko's stores, that store in Wrigleyville had the lowest average ticket size—at the time something like seven to eight dollars per ticket—and the most daily transactions, over a thousand transactions a day on average in that single store. Think about the profile of that store. You can be sure it was all people just making a copy or two for themselves, with no business traffic whatsoever. Not far away from Wrigleyville in Chicago was another Kinko's store in Lombard, Illinois, near O'Hare airport.

That store was 100 percent business-related copying and printing. The average ticket size—over $250 a ticket—was the highest in the United States, and their number of daily transactions, something around forty transactions a day, was among the lowest. Yet these two stores were in the same district and were evaluated against each other. That just didn't make sense. Wrigleyville should have been evaluated against other stores with tons of walk-in business and very low average ticket value, while the store by O'Hare should have been evaluated against a peer group of stores dominated by corporate business.

Our analysis yielded something like thirty-five separate types of store profiles. Those thirty-five types held almost all Kinko's stores, and we followed up by figuring what metrics made sense for all stores in each type. This wasn't a cost out exercise. It was a Best Demonstrated Practice and cost rationalization exercise. Yes, there were many stores that had to cut some headcount. But there were also many that had to *add* headcount. It was a best practices exercise, so that if a store in a group of similar stores had the best fax revenue, then every store in that same group would begin to use that store's fax process for driving their fax revenue. And then we did the same thing with each area of revenues from black-and-white copiers to color copiers. And from computer rental to passport photos and notary services. We knew the plan we were presenting was the mother lode of revenue generation and cost savings, but we had to get buy-in from the top leadership of the company. If we didn't make the progress these changes would generate, we would end up ousted!

Our presentation at the meeting was crisp and moved along nicely. It contained a lot of complex topics and analysis, but we felt the audience was generally understanding and thinking about the implications for their stores. The meeting was to last two days, and at the end of day one, in a question-and-answer session, a question was asked that ended up being the question whose answer would make or break our case.

The question was: "How would our President's Club stores fare in this new way of evaluating individual store performance?" That was a question that neither Dan nor I had contemplated. And it was critically important. The President's Club had been established decades before we arrived. It consisted of the elite group of the highest-performing stores in the entire Kinko's store network. There were fifty President's Club locations, and the managers of those stores had a quarterly conference call with the CEO and an annual trip with a guest to a major resort with the CEO and top officials of the company. They were the most revered people at Kinko's, the managers who operated the best and most profitable stores. The question was: Would these fifty stores still be the best performers, regardless of which store type their average ticket size and transaction numbers dictated?

I thought it was a very fair question. It seemed to me that these highly performing stores would be highly performing no matter which type of group they were part of, but I didn't know for sure. Dan and I promised the attendees that we would work all night if needed to understand where the President's Club stores would sit under this new peer group system. With knots in our stomachs and with the help of our CFO and others from the finance organization, we learned overnight that indeed *yes*, President's Club members would have virtually all remained President's Club member stores in the new system.

I can't overstate how critical that was. It validated what Dan and I had been saying all the previous day. It validated us as intellectually honest and truly working to restore Kinko's luster. It also gave Dan and me conviction—particularly me! I had to give a speech to wrap up the two-day affair. I knew that word of this conference would rocket through the twenty-five thousand team members, and based on the feedback they got, they would believe or not believe we could turn the ship around. Emboldened by the positive outcome, I decided to take a highly risky tack with my closing speech. It was one I spoke off the cuff, without notes, which no one knew was the way I have given all the talks in my life, at least those that came from my heart! Remember, this is the top 150 Kinko's senior team members of twenty-five thousand. Not the 150 senior team members I had hand selected as my team, but for the most part the team I had inherited. Many were very close friends of Paul Orfalea, the founder who had undermined CD&R at each turn, and they were fairly inclined to not like me much to start with. This is close to exactly what I said:

I appreciate having had the opportunity to spend the past two days with all of you. I know there has been severe trepidation about what might happen over these two days. But I feel like it is the right outcome. Kinko's has fallen into a very deep hole, and this feels like the first steps needed to get us a course correction back to the place where Kinko's has been before and will be again.

But I am not kidding myself. I know that there are some people in this room who fully believe I am smoking dope—that this is the dumbest thing they have ever heard and no way it will work. I hope they're wrong, but who knows at this time? What I do know is this. We all must be 100 percent aligned in believing in this plan if we are to succeed. So here is what I'm offering each of you today. For anyone here who believes this puts Kinko's on a bad course, please reach out directly to me in the next thirty days. What I promise is that I will be your best reference and will work day and night and move heaven and earth to ensure that you land on your feet in some other company, just not Kinko's.

And for any of you who do not contact me in the next thirty days, but still do not believe we are on the right path and plan to undermine our efforts from the inside, know this. I will find you, and I will personally weed you out.

You could have heard a pin drop. It was dead silent. I turned the microphone over to Dan (who probably could have killed me for giving him the microphone at that moment), who gave closing remarks and instructions and closed the meeting.

As a post mortem, three of the attendees did contact me, and all three landed on their feet. I am proud of that. I don't know if I should be, but I'm prouder of the fact that I indeed personally weeded out at least 25 percent of the attendees. The message to the company was clear. We were going to turn Kinko's around, and we were going to take no prisoners in the process. I kept in the back of my mind that the previous CEO, Joe Hardin, was a world-class executive, and the Kinko's culture chewed him up. It could do the same thing to me. I stayed on high alert for the rest of my tenure.

By rationalizing the network, moving aggressively into the very large adjacent corporate-printing businesses, and installing a highly functioning corporate-sales organization under John McDonald and Jennifer Goodwyn of HQ Global Workplaces fame, we were able to achieve so much. Kinko's earnings during the twelve months before Dan and I hit the ground were in the minus $11 million area, meaning Kinko's lost $11 million. Our first year, our profit jumped to plus $120 million. This truly monumental growth came from rationalizing the network. The second year we achieved earnings of $180 million, and the third year we were approaching $240 million in earnings due to the rapid growth of our corporate sales when we were sold.

The experiences I had at Kinko's, though crazy, certainly helped me formalize what I felt were the important leadership principles for successful companies, no matter the sector. I believe that the break-through thought, when comparing our work to what happened in other corporations, was that corporate culture was the result of executing well against other more global strategic principles. Most companies talk loudly and long about their great culture. I believe that if we all understood and bought in to a set of strong leadership principles and adhered to them, a great culture would be the result. But I had more to learn and more points to be put on the board before I was ready to talk about Leadership Principles in that way.

Meeting Paul Orfalea
and an Idea

AS I WROTE EARLIER, PAUL was a consummate entrepreneur. I knew I would like him because he was so offbeat, as are most great entrepreneurs. I also wanted to communicate to Paul that I wasn't some corporate suit and had some entrepreneurial DNA myself. By this time Paul had literally been banned from setting foot in any Kinko's stores or the corporate headquarters. There was no love lost between Paul and CD&R, and it showed. They didn't speak particularly nicely about Paul and vice versa. I had to change that if I was going to gain any traction with the changes we needed to make. Plus, I always learn the most about companies by studying history and reaching back to prior leaders when appropriate. I felt I couldn't understand Kinko's without knowing Paul.

I called Paul, and after some serious coaxing, I set up an off-site meeting with him in a restaurant in Ventura. He arrived in a pretty foul mood, as he really hated CD&R and thought I was probably in their pocket. But as I expected, we hit it off nicely. Our conversation stretched way past lunch, and then Paul ordered a bottle of wine and it went further from there. I learned so much about Paul and the history of Kinko's, information that would inform my plans going forward. We covered lots of ground, bringing us each up to speed on the other. The company truly was the "people's republic of Kinko's" for its first twenty-five years: intensely entrepreneurial and countercultural in so many ways! For instance, for the first twenty years, at each summer's company gathering in Ventura, California, just inside the entrance gate to the huge picnic was a table full of marijuana joints. That was just how it had been since the Kinko's founding in 1970. Understanding how deeply its counterculture roots ran, it became so much easier to understand the alienation brought on by private equity ownership and its attempts to make the entire Kinko's network conform to a tight set of rules built on a need for conformity. I was much more of a believer that while I had no issue with breaking glass in order to turn things around, building trust through throwing unnecessary rules overboard was a great way to start. And in pretty much record time, Paul and I developed trust.

That afternoon led to another meeting, this time at a Kinko's in Salt Lake City, Utah, in February of 2002. Kinko's was Xerox's largest customer in the world, and Xerox invited Karleen and me to go to the Winter Olympics in Salt Lake City as guests of the CEO of Xerox, Anne Mulcahy. She needed to meet and spend time with me, and I needed to meet and spend time with her, so this felt like the right kind of situation for us to enjoy and get to know each other. Ursula Burns, her second-in-command, and the sales leader who had our account, Mike McDonald, all attended. Since I was going to be there for a few days with that group, I decided I should also pop into the Kinko's locations in the marketplace to be sure they were prepared for whatever an Olympics might bring. I also thought that Salt Lake City was suitably remote that I could invite Paul back into a Kinko's store to see what was happening and share what the plan was for turning Kinko's around. Paul was fairly stunned that I was inviting him into a store, as he was still definitely persona non grata according to CD&R. I let Paul know I was in charge now and could make the call on that type of issue, and I would be delighted for him to come back into the stores.

I didn't know what to expect from Paul, though by now we were quite friendly, having spent that afternoon deep into the wine in Ventura. At that first meeting I was clear that because of the company's very bad recent results, we would have to think about the situation as very much a turnaround situation, and one in which we didn't have a lot of time to show results. Nevertheless, I was fairly shocked that as I went into detail about our turnaround plan in Salt Lake City, he agreed with virtually all of it. Frankly, I was wondering if this was some type of scam being run on me, but I finally believed he was being serious. I then made what was a very bold and/or stupid move. I invited him to come to our annual Kinko's sales meeting and surprise the entire company by walking out on the stage—if he would be willing to endorse our turnaround plan. At this point he likely thought I was working some kind of scam on him. Perfect!

Sealed with a Kiss

EACH YEAR IN THE SPRING Kinko's held a company-wide meeting where over three thousand Kinko's team members arrived at a great convention venue for meetings and selected vendor trainings. Paul and I spoke several times about what I wanted him to say at the company meeting, and he felt like he could deliver what I needed. Within Kinko's, it was an extremely small group, each sworn to secrecy, who knew what we were planning. Paul Rostron, our Kinko's head of people, who was the only member of my senior team who had been on the prior senior team, warned me about Paul Orfalea. A part of being so profoundly dyslexic was that he was very unorganized. Paul was worried that Paul a) could never stay on the topics he promised and would just ramble and b) couldn't keep his comments to a time limit. In my conversations with Paul, I kept to two thoughts. He must say whatever he and I agreed to and nothing else, and he must hold his comments to ten minutes max.

Paul was so excited to be invited back under the Kinko's tent and so happy he and I were friends that he promised me he would make me proud, that I could go over his notes in advance to see exactly what he would say and that I could put a stopwatch on him to see that he could stay inside his allotted ten minutes. Finally, he agreed that if he didn't stay inside of ten minutes, I had his permission to come on stage and remove him myself! We even choreographed his entrance. My podium was on the far left of the stage from the perspective of the audience, and he was to enter from the far right. He and I would each walk to center stage and shake hands, and then I would exit the way he walked in and he would walk to the podium to give his remarks.

The stage was set, and the secret had been kept. Virtually none of the three thousand plus team members in attendance knew what was about to happen. I gave an intro letting everyone know I had met Paul and he and I had talked over wine and again at the Olympics, and I thought we as a company needed to express again how much we all appreciated Paul for the way he had built this great company. A buzz started in the audience. What? Was Paul actually there? When I said, "Ladies and Gentlemen, Paul Orfalea," the room exploded. I don't think I had ever heard that decibel level. People jumped up screaming and yelling and even crying. Paul walked out, and we met at center stage. I stuck my hand out, and he pushed it away. Then with two hands he grabbed my face and pulled me in for a big kiss on the lips! I was stunned. He stepped back, looked at me and smiled, and headed to the podium. It was complete chaos. And I knew good and well what had just happened. He had anointed me! He had communicated to the top three thousand people at Kinko's that I was the guy and they needed to get on board.

He did live up to his billing. He pulled a stack of index cards from his pocket and told everyone he had promised to stick to the notes written on the index cards. Then he promptly dropped the cards on the floor. He got down on his hands and knees and tried to pick up the scattered cards to no avail, so he just stood up and started talking. I didn't care one iota that he spoke for thirty minutes. He said very kind things about me and about the plan we were undertaking. A lot of people mark time at Kinko's by attending either this event or by attending the event when I gave the "I will weed you out person-ally" line. Over fifteen years later I still from time to time hear from Kinko's people who remind me of either or both of those occasions.

Crossing Paths with Bill Gates Again

I FIRST MET BILL GATES sometime around 1985. He was coming through Dallas and wanted to understand our Babbage's concept since we were selling so many of the Microsoft Flight Simulators, plus he was hearing that we were also selling Microsoft productivity software well for multiple hardware platforms. During our breakfast, he was as advertised—very cerebral and definitely rocked in his seat when he was thinking. I had read about the rocking but hadn't seen it in action. All I can remember about the breakfast he and I shared was the rocking and his comment that he never would have thought about a store that mainly sold software, but he got what we were doing and it clearly was working.

Imagine my surprise when he called me at Kinko's! He had an idea he wanted to run by me. After some chitchat about GameStop, he told me that Microsoft really wanted to get into the web services business. Today we all use web services and don't even think about it, whether playing video games against players around the globe or transferring a file from a desktop to another person or business anywhere in the world. But in 2003 it was a pretty big idea! Bill's thought was this: that he and I would put on a skit at the annual Consumer Electronics Show in Las Vegas to illustrate his concept. He would be himself, trying to get a proposal to a person in another city. He would be stranded, wondering how he would do that—and, of course, Kinko's would come to the rescue. I would come onstage in my Kinko's apron and explain to him that he could transfer his file to our Kinko's website, and we would print it in whatever city he wished and deliver it for him wherever he wished.

Bill was sure this was an example everyone could understand, and obviously I was happy to play along. While we rehearsed, I asked him why he kept twirling a paper clip in his fingers. He told me he had attention deficit disorder, and twirling the paper clip while talking served to help him stay focused and on point. It triggered a thought that maybe his rocking in a chair when talking served the same purpose for him. As an ADD person myself, with my ADD genes reaching down through my children to my grandchildren, it was very comforting for me to learn that Bill Gates had the same disorder. When I have tried that trick since, it has also worked for me, but I have developed my own tricks over the years to keep myself focused during presentations and longer speeches. Because I am a visual person and don't really learn from slides or pages in a book, I have built a method that works for me. It has three steps. The first is to think about what I want to say. I do that in very large brushstrokes in my head. The next step is to think about how I want to say it. At that point I write sort of an outline—which is when I put my thoughts on paper for the first time. The third and final step is converting that outline of what I want to say into, literally, a road map, complete with twists and turns. Then I just pretend I'm driving down the road, which has twists and turns based on my outline, and talk with my brain visualizing the map. My mouth handles everything else! That works for me better than a paper clip. If my brain worked as well as Bill's, I probably could keep what is in my head on a paper clip. The good news is that the skit was a huge success, and Kinko's got an incredible amount of editorial press from it. Plus, Bill and I really enjoyed doing that together.

Beginning a year later, I was invited to what I learned was an annual event that Bill hosted for one hundred CEOs from around the world. Fifty CEOs were from the United States and the remaining fifty were from outside the United States. I was in a very rarified atmosphere for those three days, and Bill invited me to three straight CEO events over the following years. Everyone brought significant others, so Karleen was there to enjoy the festivities with me during the three years we took part in his annual event. The event ended the last night with all the CEOs and significant others having dinner at his home—which was spectacular. His library had first editions and originals of manuscripts you assumed would be in the Library of Congress. All the CEOs there were a little humbled by what they saw. There is always a bigger fish! That is the big lesson. As an aside and to underscore that thought, Bill owned the Getty Images company, so he owned the digital rights to most of the great art across history. If it was just an individual coming to dinner at his home, and Bill happened to know that guest liked Monet, for instance, when the guest arrived, all the frames in the house would be showing digital representations of Monet's art. When a docent who was showing us the electronics that powered his house told our large group about the digital ownership and how they used technology to transmit images to frames on walls, I asked how much bandwidth Bill needed in his house to be able to do what he was doing. He said, "Well, what I can tell you is that there is more wiring in this home than in a Boeing 777 airliner." Me, being me, responded, "How could that be? There almost certainly can't be that much wiring here." He leaned in to me and said, "I'm the chief engineer at Boeing. I know the exact wiring of a 777, and I know the exact wiring of this house. I designed the electronics in this house." Talk about shutting me down fast in front of a pretty powerful group!

Francis Ford Coppola Calling

I *LOVED* BEING CEO OF Kinko's. By 2003 we had over 98 percent name recognition in the United States. For comparison, FedEx had 99 percent name recognition. And we had over a million transactions a week in our stores. We were really part of the woodwork in America. It wasn't unusual to see us in a skit on *Saturday Night Live*. Some crazy stuff would come my way on a fairly regular basis. None was crazier than the call I got one afternoon from Francis Ford Coppola. I had the obvious reaction when Traci Walters, my extremely capable assistant, walked into my office and told me who was on the line. I couldn't imagine what he wanted with me, and I doubted it was really him, but I took the call. He introduced himself and asked if he could get a meeting set with me to discuss one of his projects. I felt there was some chance it was him, since his looks were so unique and no one could dare come into my office masquerading as him.

We set a date, and at the designated time he came into my office with a case of wine under his arm from his vineyard in Napa. He had a tie on but still looked disheveled, as I had always seen him in photos. I had Dan Connors and Tom Leverton, who was Dan's number two in his organization, join me for the meeting, as they were generally in charge of all new business development. Plus, they were both huge fans of Coppola. It turned out that he owned a company named Zoetrope, which had workshops for writers, directors, and other creative people to develop their ideas. The company also produced a corporate magazine named *Zoetrope*. Francis felt that if we could dedicate a bit of each Kinko's store to a "Zoetrope Corner" for creative artists to gather for the same purpose, but on a distributed basis across one thousand plus locations, it could really accelerate the creative process for the film industry. I couldn't even spell Zoetrope and didn't have Francis's vision, but Dan and Tom jumped right in with really smart questions and observations. They were trying to understand the market size for Zoetrope, along with the number of people who could utilize that service and how geographically dispersed they were. The conversation was so refreshing for him that Coppola invited Dan and Tom to travel to Napa Valley and stay on his property for a weekend. Of course, Dan and Tom jumped at the opportunity, and they had what each described later as a lifetime experience staying at his home and enjoying his hospitality for the weekend. At the end of the day, we couldn't spare even a corner of the floor space in each store and weren't sure it would really be used for the intended purpose, so we passed on that opportunity.

OMG! Jack Welch Quarterly Business Reviews

JACK WELCH, WHO IS CONSIDERED one of the top business leaders in the twentieth century by virtually every measure, had been the CEO of General Electric for decades, and under his leadership GE had become one of the most highly valued companies in the world. He was most famous for his GE quarterly business reviews, where, in front of the entire top leadership team of each of his divisions, he would review the results and dig deeply into those results to discern what was the right next strategic or operational step if it wasn't obvious. He would get commitments on what would be delivered by the next quarterly business review, and the next quarter he would show up like clockwork and the management team had better have delivered whatever they had promised!

When Jack retired, he quickly jumped into CD&R as an operating partner. Rather than have specific companies to oversee like other operating partners, he ran quarterly business reviews for CD&R's largest and/or most troubled investments. Kinko's qualified on both measures, at least early in my tenure. As I prepared for my first business review with Jack, I wondered if he could really be as good as his press. I decided that there was only a remote chance he was that good, so when I went into my first-ever meeting with him, I already felt a bit jaded about how I might receive his input. Wow! Was I wrong! Even today I am still not sure what hit me. I put a slide on the wall about our large commercial sales organization, and he stopped my description of the slide and started asking questions about our large corporate sales organization. What was its account composition, salesperson compensation plan with commission structure, average salesperson total account revenue size, etc., along with what were the margins in the large corporate business space versus our consumer business and small and medium-size businesses? By the end of that session, I had entirely new marching orders, not only related to how to organize the commercial sales organization differently but, more importantly, how to compensate the sales team differently to maximize their performance. It was a stunning virtuoso performance by Jack. And each quarter for probably the next six quarters we had those meetings, I learned an array of lessons of major importance to my growth as a CEO that for Jack were almost throwaway lines.

Interestingly enough, Jack's greatest lessons for me were gems tucked into private lunches or drinks in the corner before larger dinners. Jack thrived in one-on-one meetings. On one occasion I voiced my chagrin at having hired eight new senior officers at Kinko's after I had fired thirteen of the fourteen direct reports of my predecessor. I shared that within twelve to eighteen months I had actually fired four of the eight people I had hired. I was feeling pretty crappy about that and wondered if he had any insight. He shared that, statistically, batting .500 is average in large corporations relative to success in hiring, and that I shouldn't beat myself up about that. I then asked if he had any advice for firing people, and he really lit up. He was a fanatic about open and honest conversations. He told me he considered it a failure if he ever fired someone who was surprised. He said the key was communication, especially at performance reviews. He reviewed his typical talk track, which was to remind the team member that all the financial plans roll to the top of the company, where they are reviewed by the board of directors and approved. The company is expected to meet its financial obligations every year. If one of Jack's reports turns in a financial plan that it misses, it means that Jack's financial plan will miss, even if everyone else meets their targets. So Jack can't have any of his direct reports turn in budget numbers they won't meet. And he lets the person know that in the next fiscal year budget he really must hit his budget commitment and that he simply can't miss two in a row. Then the next year if he does miss his budget commitment, Jack reminds the person of their prior year conversation. He then tells the team member how much he likes them, reminds the person of golf outings or when he met the person's spouse or kids, and then says that as much as he likes the person, they simply can't stay since they can't hit the budgetary commitments. Jack believed it was critical to separate the termination from the person as much as possible. Getting fired is traumatic enough that it has to be done gently.

Frankly, his next piece of advice is something I have used ever since. He starts termination meetings by saying he is about to have a very difficult conversation with the person. That immediately gets the 100 percent focus of the person and gives them a chance to gird themselves for the conversation. That advice, in particular, has held me in good stead. And it underscores how critical honesty and integrity are, especially in the most difficult conversations. I will treasure those sessions as having been visits to the business mountain with Jack Welch.

Key Lessons

PART 6

Harness Past Experiences:

Every role you've played has prepared you for future challenges. Draw from your history to navigate present complexities.

Embrace Change as a Catalyst:

Change is the engine of progress. Embrace it wholeheartedly, even when it feels uncomfortable.

Trust in the Power of Relationships:

Relationships, not transactions, drive enduring success. Invest in people genuinely and the dividends will be manifold.

Cultivate an Entrepreneurial Spirit:

Foster a culture of innovation and risk-taking. The entrepreneurial spirit is the lifeline of a vibrant company.

Leadership Transcends Boundaries:

Your influence should reach beyond the confines of the boardroom, resonating with the front-line employees and the broader community.

Engage with Transparency and Integrity:

In all dealings, whether negotiating exits or new beginnings, act with unassailable integrity.

Recognize the Importance of Timing:

Decisions are not just about *what* but also about *when*.
Timing can be the difference between success and failure.

Leverage Your Scale Wisely:

Understand your organization's breadth and use it to create
systems and processes that drive efficiency and cohesion.

Value Culture as Your Compass:

Corporate culture isn't just part of the game—it is the game.
Nurture it as you would your most valuable asset.

Communicate with Clarity and Conviction:

Whether it's a rallying cry or a difficult message, clear and
confident communication is key.

Prioritize Honesty in Feedback:

Honest feedback is a gift. Cherish it, provide it generously,
and examine it with respect and the intent to foster growth.

Be a Custodian of the Company's Legacy:

Respect the past as you innovate for the future. Honor
the foundation upon which your company was built while
paving new paths.

Measure Twice, Cut Once:

In decision making, be thorough. Analyze each angle twice,
ensuring that when action is taken, it's precise and decisive.

PART SEVEN

PUTTING IT ALL TOGETHER

Fred Smith Walks through My Door

KINKO'S HAD A GREAT RELATIONSHIP with FedEx over the years leading up to my joining the company. In fact, when I joined Kinko's, five hundred of the twelve hundred Kinko's stores had staffed FedEx drop locations in place. That means that anyone wanting to drop off anything for FedEx could just run into one of the five hundred Kinko's and hand off their package to a FedEx employee, and the package would be on its way. It was a great convenience for our customers, and FedEx paid us rent and provided their own counter, so it was a win-win-win. FedEx got lots of packages at each Kinko's (at that time we didn't know how many or if they were happy with that number or not!), our customers got a convenient, free service for coming into our stores, and Kinko's got more traffic than they would have without FedEx and rental income from some of the underutilized floor space.

Annually FedEx would send in one of its top people to discuss the past year's business and talk about other ways we could work better and/or differently together, so it wasn't a surprise for me when I learned that Mike Glenn, the global leader of marketing for FedEx at the time, was planning a trip to Dallas and wanted to meet privately with me to discuss the business. Meeting privately was a surprise, and I wondered what that could mean. By that time, we were being actively courted by and in conversations with Office Depot, Staples, and Pitney Bowes about possible business combinations, and I wondered if FedEx had gotten wind of that. Our results were exceedingly good, and CD&R was trying to measure market appetite to sell us. We were doing our part, and Dan Connors, as usual, was spearheading a terrific effort to create compelling decks about the power of the Kinko's network. As the meeting time grew near, we got a message that Mike was going to bring someone else and then later that no, he wasn't going to bring someone. He was going to come alone.

At the appointed time, who should walk into my office but FedEx founder Fred Smith, alone. I was pretty stunned but kept my composure, as I really didn't know the purpose of the visit. I had seen photos of Fred over my business career, as he was such a business icon with a superior reputation. FedEx had proposed a number of ways to expand our relationship in the past, and I thought perhaps he was upset that we had not made any additional agreements on my watch. I also knew that FedEx was obsessed with UPS Stores. Though UPS Stores was a franchise organization, it had thousands of locations and extended the UPS brand nicely. I can't remember the preliminary chatter, but I definitely remember the core conversation. It went something like this:

Fred: Gary, today we have about five hundred staffed FedEx locations inside of Kinko's stores. Altogether, including those five hundred locations, we have more than one thousand staffed FedEx locations in the United States. Did you know that the worst Kinko's location of the five hundred Kinko's FedEx locations, literally number five hundred of the Kinko's locations, is still the number five hundred location of the more than one thousand total FedEx staffed locations? Your stores generate an enormous number of packages for FedEx every day. That is a little fun fact for you.

Gary: Wow! I had no idea!

Fred: Yes, and you can imagine how hard we compete with UPS stores. We believe if we were in all Kinko's stores and added packing and shipping services, we could win head-to-head against UPS stores. What would you say about combining Kinko's with FedEx? [I knew I was moving into uncharted territory, as I had absolutely no authority to even enter into negotiations to sell Kinko's without CD&R's 100 percent involvement. Undeterred, I plowed ahead!]

Gary: I think that would make a lot of sense. But we're really doing well, and I know that CD&R would require at least ten times EBITDA.

Fred: I completely understand that, and bet I would want ten times EBITDA also. Tell me what your current EBITDA will be this year.

Gary: We are tracking to $240 million of EBITDA.

Fred: So CD&R would be looking for $2.4 billion for selling Kinko's. [He looked up at the ceiling and reflected for a moment.] Yes, we could pay that.

Gary: [Thinking, how do I backtrack off this since I can't be having this conversation.] Fred, I know these guys, and I know they would want a fast close.

Fred: What would they think about a ninety-day close.

Gary: That would be great, but I also know they would want all cash.

Fred: I guess that's all right also. We could do all cash. Anything else?

Gary: [Perhaps sweating a bit.] No, I think that would cover it.

We actually shook hands! And then, without me asking any questions, he said, "My request for you is this. I would like you to remain as CEO of the new FedEx Kinko's company for two full years. For those two years I will want you on my SMC, the Strategic Management

Committee that manages FedEx globally. You will report directly to
me. We will pay you what you're making now, and we'll give you your
own FedEx SMC plane with three crew members, a mechanic, and a
scheduler based in Dallas. We'll ask you to use the plane for all FedEx
and personal flying and just try to keep it to one hundred hours or less
of flying a year."

I was dying—was this an IQ test or was Fred trying to sell past
the close? As I learned, he really wanted me happy and was doing all
he could to accomplish that. He didn't know he had me at $2.4 billion,
all cash, and ninety days to close! When he left, I sat back down at
my desk and then got up and closed the door. I took a deep breath
and called Don Gogel, the CEO of CD&R. I was pretty sure the call
would go sideways quickly until I got to the punchline. I decided to
have some fun.

<u>Gary</u>: Hi Don. I wanted to give you a call and let you know I just sold
  Kinko's. Even shook on it!
<u>Don</u>: [Laughing] Yeah, sure. What's going on?
<u>Gary</u>: Seriously, Don. Fred Smith just walked out of my office, and we
  shook hands on the deal.
<u>Don</u>: [A few choice words that are unprintable, but all having to do
  with the fact that I had no authority to do that and why hadn't I
  called George and what was going on in Dallas?]
<u>Gary</u>: Don, would you like to know the deal?
<u>Don</u>: Yes.
<u>Gary</u>: $2.4 billion. All cash. Ninety days to close. That was it.
<u>Don</u>: Bullshit!
<u>Gary</u>: Nope, I swear! [I had paused to check what the stock price
  would be at $2.4 billion. It would be $38.11 a share for a stock
  worth $7 a share when I joined Kinko's. I told him that too.]
<u>Don</u>: Unbelievable! Congratulations!

We then spent time talking through how we would insert CD&R into the process, which was easy. And FedEx lived up to Fred's promise and our handshake. Over the long Thanksgiving weekend, a huge team from Memphis spent the holiday weekend at our empty offices going through our books. They cleared the transaction, and on December 29, 2004, it was publicly announced that FedEx had bought Kinko's. The press onslaught was crazy and didn't stop for the next few days. Fred did most of the talking, but I had fun in the interviews also. And Fred and I created a bond that lasted for the next two years—it was magical.

Reasons Why Kinko's Was My Best Career Stop Ever

SOMETIMES THE STARS JUST LINE up, and my Kinko's experience was surely one of those times. As it ended up, at fifty years old when I joined Kinko's, I had the exact background that prepared me best in order to turn Kinko's around. I was an entrepreneur myself and totally sympathetic to the rank-and-file team members, which was a big change from the prior CEO. And it was such a fortuitous merging of events that brought Paul Orfalea and me together. That kiss truly did seal the deal with the team members about the potential of the plan. And of course, Dan Connors was a rock star of the highest order. But really there were a couple of other outcomes that I haven't forgotten and still make me so proud and happy when I think about them today.

First, anytime there is a successful company, most of the senior team will get great offers to take their career to a new level. We were no exception at Kinko's. I am so proud of the number of CEOs who came out of our Kinko's turnaround management team. We must have been doing something right! A short, not all-inclusive list, but the best my foggy brain can deliver at this point, of team members who became CEOs includes Dan Connors, Render Dahiya, Jennifer Goodwyn, Mark Blinn, Tom Leverton, Joe Luongo, Charlie Morrison, Chris Ahearn, John McDonald, and Flynn Decker. That's probably some sort of record in business for one company in three short years to turn out so many CEOs!

Second, it also makes me very proud how many team members earned so much money from the sale to FedEx, and I credit that 100 percent to Paul Orfalea's original vision of rank-and-file team members having "a fraction of the action." When CD&R bought out all the regional owners of Kinko's, they didn't buy out the store managers, most of whom stayed during the years until the buyout by FedEx. We had hundreds of store managers who each earned hundreds of thousands of dollars, and district managers who made up to ten times that much. And so on! Plenty of the team earned millions each. I am so proud of the depth into the organization that the sale dollars managed to touch. It stands as a middle finger salute from Paul Orfalea, who had created that stock ownership plan that penetrated all the way to the store manager level.

Finally, just a story that illustrates the above. About ten years ago, well over a decade after I left Kinko's, Karleen and I had boarded a plane heading somewhere and were sitting in our seats. As the line of people boarding was going slowly, I looked up to see a person staring intently at me. He said, "Gary! You won't remember me from Kinko's, though we spent time together at various company events. I'm so happy to see you. Do you mind if I hug you? I have always told myself that if I ever saw you, I would hug you. My family made so much money at the sale to FedEx that I was able to pay off the mortgage on our house, put my kids through college, and save for my retirement. And it was because of that turnaround. You made us all believe it could be done, so we went out and did it. It was the high point of my career!" You can't imagine how fast I jumped up and hugged this person. I was so moved, and Karleen was too. What a validation of what we had accomplished!

I had myself a little cry while that flight was taking off. That, for me, is what life is all about.

And, oh, by the way, the sale was such an incredible home run that I bought all the CD&R partners involved with Kinko's and every Kinko's team member who reported to me a pair of custom-made boots from Leddy's Western Store in Fort Worth. Each person selected the skin they wanted for their boots, along with every other detail when they got their feet measured. The boots were shipped to each person when they were ready about a year later. Inside each boot there is a logo. The FedEx logo is inside one boot, and the Kinko's logo is inside the other. They were just a little reminder for each member of the team who worked so hard and succeeded with such a great transaction. You wouldn't believe how fast those CD&R partners were on a plane to Dallas to pick out their boots. There are always all sorts of "deal toys" available when deals are consummated, but I bet few rivaled those boots! And my boots from that transaction remain my favorite boots ever.

Wait a Second! My Two Years at FedEx Were My Best Ever

WELL, I GUESS I CAN'T make up my mind whether the three years of the Kinko's turnaround or the two years with FedEx were best. I think my ambivalence comes from the fact that my three years at Kinko's were such hard work, with a 24/7 knot in my stomach, worried that things wouldn't work. My next two years reporting to Fred Smith were a walk in the park. I had been paid at the close of the transaction, so I had true wealth for the first time in my life. I wasn't worried about being fired, as I had an easy job to do, and I was doing it well, and I *loved, loved, loved* my one-on-one time with Fred. Those Fridays when I joined him for a private meeting in his Memphis office after the regular SMC meetings were so special. Fred is such a smart man, and beyond that he is so intellectually curious. He always had lots of questions for me about an array of things he was thinking and wondering about and vice versa. We had a casual, relaxed relationship, which I know he enjoyed, as the intensity of the SMC meetings was very real. He managed the way a lifelong entrepreneur who had created one of the best-known brands in the world would manage. He didn't suffer fools. He expected people to deliver on the commitments they made, and as a result FedEx was an incredibly highly functioning and extraordinarily successful company.

How we changed the name from Kinko's to FedEx Kinko's and finally to FedEx Office is a telling story, with a funny aside that really illustrates both why I could never, ever work at FedEx other than for the time and duty I had, but also why Fred and I liked each other so much.

I had learned in the FedEx SMC meetings that the power of package drops at Kinko's was important not just for its number of packages—something like 3 percent of US FedEx packages in their network came through Kinko's stores daily—but also because the margin of the packages dropped at Kinko's stores was extraordinary. FedEx made its highest margins on product dropped at Kinko's locations because most people coming into Kinko's didn't have an account with FedEx, which means they didn't get any discounts on the price they paid for the packages they shipped through FedEx. If you did the math, which I learned later, the margins FedEx made through Kinko's were so high that they didn't really have to be concerned about the copy and print revenues and didn't even care if the copy revenues went to zero. All that mattered is that FedEx could add packaging services and other FedEx services that fit more with the FedEx system than what fit into Kinko's system. That was proven correct after the name was changed to FedEx Office, and copy and print revenue began slumping. Without Kinko's in the name, some customers wondered if FedEx Office even offered printing, and if they did, was it the Kinko's quality product? That ended up not being a problem, as the package revenues soared, far exceeding copy and print revenues.

There was a big question at FedEx about how long and how many iterations it might take to move from a company called Kinko's to a company called FedEx Office. To that end they hired one of the top branding firms in America to help them with that decision. Among things they learned was that while FedEx had name recognition with 99 percent of Americans, Kinko's was not far behind at all, with name recognition among 98 percent of Americans. FedEx was nothing if not an "academy" company, simply one of the best-managed firms in the world, with prestige that FedEx surely thought separated it from "the people's republic of Kinko's," known for its offbeat founder and as a very laid-back company. FedEx likely cringed to learn that only 1 percent name recognition separated an academy company from a, well, let us say *not* academy company!

When this big-time branding firm pitched their belief that we should quickly change the name to FedEx Kinko's and then at a later date change to FedEx Office, I asked Fred, once the marketing firm left the SMC meeting, how much FedEx had paid for that work. Corporate politics being what it is, with everyone so protective of their turf, my questions were usually not very politic, and clearly this question wasn't either. No doubt I wasn't considered very genteel, as people in Memphis tend to be. I just say what is on my mind and let the chips fall where they may. Most of the SMC members looked at me sideways, especially the head of marketing, who promptly said $3 million. I laughed and said, "Fred, if you would have just asked me, I would have charged you only $2 million and given you the exact same answer." Fred burst out laughing, and I got very ugly stares from most of the others. I had clearly never been involved with a company of the size, scope, and prestige of FedEx, much less one with such a powerful and intelligent founder at the wheel.

It was a rare treat for me to see up close and personal how things are done at one of the top academy companies in America. By now I was fifty-three years old with a varied career full of new experiences under my belt. FedEx was a thing of beauty for a person like me, who had the DNA of an entrepreneur with a love for learning. But I was no longer a naive young person, without answers and just trying to understand the questions. I had confidence born from thirty years of managing, thinking, and staring out airplane windows. Instead of waking up to a new world every day, I was waking up to a world more like *Groundhog Day*. I was much more apt to see a pattern emerging that I had seen before, so my batting average for picking the right outcome had dramatically improved from when I was a young boy playing mind games with the world around me. I was learning the power of pattern recognition and had gained enough confidence to be willing to stick my chin out and formulate questions that could help guide the person I was conversing with to get to an answer that might work for them. At FedEx, certainly I learned that I would have failed miserably in a command-and-control work environment and would have hated the experience all along the way. It simply wasn't who I was. But I loved my time getting that education.

Decision to Go Into Private Equity

I BELIEVED THAT WHEN I left FedEx I would probably retire. While I hadn't been thinking about retirement, I couldn't figure out why I would work. I was in entirely new territory. I'd had to work from my adolescent years up until this point. There was a family to raise and mouths to feed. I worked because I had to, plain and simple. And all of a sudden, at fifty-five years old, I didn't have to work. The experience Karleen and I had with the facilitator, developing a seven-word mission statement based on the seven months, seven weeks, seven days construct, came in the middle of my decision making, so I had the advantage of realizing that I cared most deeply about learning and teaching.

Recruiting firms were calling with CEO openings all over the world. While I wasn't interested in being a CEO any longer, a Bain senior partner I had worked with extensively had called me, wanting to talk about the private equity firm Texas Pacific Group (TPG), led by David Bonderman, Jim Coulter, and Bill Price. It was located in Fort Worth and San Francisco. The Bain partner thought that PE would be a good landing spot for me and that if I was interested in private equity, he believed there was a perfect situation for me at TPG. He said my personality and style fit that group very well. Plus, he thought I would love meeting the team at TPG and vice versa. I said great, and off I went to San Francisco. He was correct; everyone I met at TPG passed my dinner test. That test is pretty simple: would you want to sit next to them at a nice dinner? So many people I had met along my journey had failed that test. TPG was interested in having me join their firm, so I asked them if there was a process by which I could temporarily join a TPG team conducting due diligence on a target company. By doing that, I could see how the teams worked and get a feel for what the culture was at TPG. We decided on Michaels Stores because it was based in Dallas, it was a very big deal (over a $3 billion acquisition if we acquired), and it had a good TPG team just kicking off due diligence.

At the same time, Clayton, Dubilier & Rice also called. Because they knew me from Kinko's and had shared the spectacular success, they thought I would be a great candidate to join their firm as a partner, and it would be something that would interest me. I asked them for the same opportunity as TPG had extended, to join a due diligence team where I might learn how the process worked on their side of the deal table. They were just starting due diligence on Sally Beauty, based in Denton, Texas. I joined that due diligence team, so overnight I was working concurrently with two very different PE firms on private equity due diligence teams, reviewing Sally Beauty and Michaels Stores, both based in and around Dallas.

Because of the seven-month, seven-week, seven-day, and seven-word facilitated event I had just completed, I indeed made my decision to pursue private equity. The primary reason is that it played to both my desire for learning opportunities and engaged my pattern recognition by presenting so many different types of business situations. I was correct. I likely got an up-close-and-personal look at between four and seven global businesses a year that I would never have learned about otherwise. Examples include a mattress manufacturer in Norway, a superstore opening in India, and a specialty apparel company based in Northern England. Each scratched my itch to learn about new and interesting things. One of my responsibilities if we succeeded in making an acquisition was to become a mentor to the CEO, along with other board duties. I was able to learn and teach as part of my job description. There are so many types of businesses and cultures in the world that I had not experienced, and being part of due diligence teams globally would satisfy my desire to learn. There was no question in my mind that private equity would be my next stop. And there was no question that TPG was the place I wanted to hang my hat for my next chapter. Being around such a smart and collegial group was a benefit I felt I had earned. Also, Caroline was starting college in Northern California, so being close to her was a huge plus for Karleen and me. We could see her on a regular basis. I had my decision!

The TPG Years

WORKING AT TPG WAS LIKE drinking through a fire hose. I loved that I could learn all day every day, especially given the fact that I wasn't also "carrying the keys" as a CEO. The buck stops squarely with the CEO 100 percent of the time for everything in a company. For twenty-three straight years I had carried the keys as a cofounder, president, chairman, or CEO of multiple companies. It was a duty I lived with 24/7/52, on vacation or not, as do all CEOs. To not carry the keys was as much of a relief to me as had been my two years integrating Kinko's into FedEx. I really never knew how much I hated carrying the keys until I got to work without that additional responsibility. At TPG there is a process for everything, steps that case teams must step through in sequence to get a target company from an investment idea to a completed investment. That made it fun for me, as I have also become a process guy.

I was learning so much that I was almost in overload mode. And the teams I worked with were such great human beings—smart as they could be and fun to travel and work with. Dick Boyce was my boss, I think. I didn't fit on a normal organization chart. We partnered on a bunch of things, but he definitely oversaw my operating work. And

I was pretty much attached at the hip with Carrie Wheeler on all new businesses in the consumer and retail areas for all the years I was at TPG. Carrie was the head of the consumer and retail investment group during my TPG tenure. We looked at more potential deals than I can remember, and we worked so well together. I was the Will Rogers of Carrie's investment team—I never met an investment I didn't like! Carrie was obviously more balanced in her analysis, which is, of course, why she had her position! It was so much fun discussing new opportunities and the investment possibilities with such a smart person as Carrie. I think we both felt that we had covered all the bases after we had finished reviewing a company.

My experience as a CEO definitely made me a valuable member of the various due diligence teams. Pattern recognition was a much-needed component of most due diligence teams, given the youth of most team members on those teams, especially compared to me with my varied experiences. Those experiences had given me a relatively good sense of pattern recognition for sure. When facts started stacking up in one direction, I could often see where the facts would likely end up before they actually ended up there. One unexpected example of the value of my pattern recognition showed up quite quickly. With my extensive CEO background, I have seen plenty of both good and bad interpersonal dynamics within various organizations. I was able in one instance to, at the first due diligence meeting, note the horrible senior team chemistry, complete with crossed arms when one person spoke, eye rolls when other officers spoke, and other indications. At one point, six of the nine people sitting in front of us had their arms crossed and chairs pushed back from the table! That was a sure sign of trouble that others missed. They just didn't know what to look for. It had come with all the experiences in my career, which more junior people hadn't encountered.

I did get to choose the TPG businesses where I wanted to spend time and contribute, which was a luxury for me. Perhaps most importantly, because I spent huge amounts of time with the younger members at the firm on due diligence teams, I got to know many of them very well. These were graduates from the top schools who were recruited by all the major PE firms around the country. As a rule, each had an enormous amount of intellectual curiosity and often would bring me their issues for advice and input. I played an important role for them, as they knew they could come to me with issues at TPG without worrying about any confidentiality breaches.

It took me a few years to really understand how things worked at TPG. It was all very logical and made great sense, but it was a new industry for me. I will focus on four investments in which I was involved during the due diligence review process and then with board responsibility once we completed the acquisition.

Petco was the first investment in which I worked on the due diligence team and then joined the board once the transaction closed. TPG and Leonard Green Partners had together owned Petco years before and had taken it public. Petco then fell on hard times as a public company, so TPG and LGP took them private again. And I joined the board the second time it became a private company. This was my first involvement as a senior adviser and board member. I probably came on a little too strong because I still had CEO juices coursing through my veins and my pattern recognition was telling me that the senior management didn't have the energy to do what would be required. With the permission of both TPG and LGP, I began pushing the fine CEO to bring in new talent in all the important positions in order to make a run at becoming a more highly functioning organization. I was pleasantly surprised that the CEO was so amenable. But he was a pro, and I helped him interview all key hires as he transformed the senior team. We then focused on developing private label programs from China to improve our assortments and our margins. He hired a team from McKinsey that was perfect for the assignment. Almost everything we tried worked, and the results improved tremendously.

Myer Department Stores in Australia. If there ever was a perfect opportunity for me to contribute to TPG, it was this investment. Myer was the biggest department store in Australia, and TPG had a deep practice in global department stores. I had helped look at Debenhams in England and saw other due diligence reports from other teams working on department stores in China and Germany, but Myer was special. I'm not sure why this is true, but the first time I ever walked into a Myer store, it was as if I had stepped into a time warp and back into Sanger-Harris in 1980. The layout, the signage, the lighting, the analytics: everything was vintage 1980s United States. They had one more upscale competitor, but Myer was beloved by its customer base across Australia.

I had become a more proper senior adviser by the time of my Myer assignment and wasn't heavy-handed, as I had been at Petco. I think my advice was eventually welcome. I was able to teach them how to use GMROI as a tool to determine what products should go in which areas of the store. GMROI is computed by multiplying gross margin by inventory turnover. The punchline on GMROI is simply that how fast an item sells is much more important than the margin of the item sold. Think about the painter's pants in Sacramento. We may have had a rack that held seventy-two pairs of painter's pants. Now imagine selling out that entire rack each week, which is what we did for months! So we turned over the rack weekly—which works out to fifty-two turns a year. And imagine the jeans had a 40 percent gross margin. That means that if the jeans have a $100 price point, each pair that sells delivers $40 of margin to the retailer. GMROI would be .40 (40 percent gross margin) times fifty-two (times a year that everything sells out on that rack). That is .40 times 52 = 20.8 GMROI. Now consider that washing machine that sells for $1,000 once every two weeks at 20 percent gross margin. That is .20 times 26. That GMROI is 5.2, versus 20.8 for the jeans. There is no comparison between the value of high-margin apparel that turns over quickly versus low-margin appliances that turn much less often. GMROI is simply an illustrator of a truth, a proxy for the value the items have on their floor space. You want your products with the highest GMROI in the very best locations on the floor where the most customers can see them.

The introduction of GMROI by itself was a big deal, and the floor allocations changed dramatically. But there were also adjacencies that hadn't ever been considered. For instance, from where I sat in my car in a parking garage next to one of their stores, I had a straight view into the women's intimate apparel department, which was positioned right next to appliances! It was very easy to illustrate the issues with having intimate apparel in such an open environment, with a clear line of sight from the parking garage, and it was easier yet to explain why it doesn't make sense to place a very high GMROI category like intimate apparel right next to one of the lowest GMROI categories in the entire store. I felt good about what I was learning and teaching on that assignment; Myer turned around nicely, and we were able to take it public successfully.

Next was TXU Energy, which TPG, KKR, and Goldman Sachs joined forces to acquire in 2007. Because it was based in Dallas and was a huge investment that would require a lot of work, I was drafted early to join the deal team to see where I could help. TXU Energy was involved in three businesses: a) Luminant, a subsidiary company involved in energy generation through a large fleet of power generation plants, both fossil fuel and nuclear power, b) transmission and distribution of energy through its Oncor subsidiary that moved power across the power lines around the state, and c) retail distribution of energy through its retail TXU Energy subsidiary, which was the entity that individual homes and businesses contracted with for their electricity needs. This investment was a very big deal to TPG, KKR, and Goldman Sachs, and for each firm, it was one of the biggest dollar investments ever. It was a monster transaction and very high profile. It was determined that my highest and best use would be on the board of

directors of the TXU Energy subsidiary and on the Comanche Peak
Nuclear Power Plant oversight committee. Thus began my up-close-
and-personal education with fossil fuels and nuclear power, including
how states determine the ways they will deliver energy to their citizens.
I also attended conferences led by the Nuclear Regulatory Commission
(NRC) on how to be a good member of a nuclear oversight committee.
An interesting tidbit: it's easy to wonder how I might find myself on
the oversight committee of a major nuclear power plant. The reason
is simple! The NRC requires every nuclear power plant in America
to have its own nuclear power oversight committee, and by law, one
member of each committee needs to be a person with no prior knowledge of nuclear power but a member in good standing of the business
community served by the plant. The thought was that a businessperson,
while perhaps not well schooled at all in nuclear power, knows what
a well-run, highly functioning organization should look like and can
be first to call out items considered issues. Even the NRC understood
the power of pattern recognition!

I truly enjoyed my time in those two roles, especially getting
to know Jim Burke, the CEO of TXU Energy. He was just a perfect CEO, in my opinion, and I learned the electric utility business
from Jim, from power generation in coal-driven plants to power from
nuclear power plants and wind power, along with the economics of
each. I learned about transmission and distribution of power from the
generator to the neighborhoods where users live and then how the electricity was priced in a highly competitive marketplace. As a member of
the TXU Energy subsidiary board, I was invited to attend the overall
corporate board meetings, which were also great learning experiences.
David Bonderman sat on that board, along with top KKR partners and
Goldman Sachs partners. But we also had two other board members
of the highest order. Don Evans, who was the former US secretary
of commerce under President George W. Bush, and Secretary James
Baker III, a US secretary of state who had served multiple presidents

in top roles. Just being in a room with Secretary Baker was a privilege beyond compare. I made it a priority to finagle a seat at the lunch table during board lunches just to listen to him speak. What a legend! I feel so privileged to have spent time with him.

My other board duty, due to where I lived, was Sabre Holdings. TPG and Silver Lake Partners bought Sabre Holdings in 2007. Sabre was a much smaller company than TXU Energy, but it was very expensive, with very high upside. TPG and Silver Lake decided that my role would be to bring some "adult supervision" to the board of directors. As they told me, because of my proximity to the company it would be easy for me to stop in should circumstances warrant. Sabre Holdings makes the software that fuels the travel industry. They make reservation software for airlines, hotels, and travel agencies. Plus, they make software that helps airlines schedule their planes, their pilots, and their services. Sabre spun out of American Airlines early in the 2000s. I joined the board in 2007 and rolled off the board in 2022 after fifteen years. It was a great assignment, and several issues surfaced during my tenure in which my prior work experience informed the right approach. I was able to accomplish some things during that tenure that I am very proud of, and I especially treasure some friendships I made along the way. It was just another example of what can happen when really smart people lean into problems and solve what many may have thought to be intractable.

My best lessons from the thirteen years at TPG ultimately reinforced what I knew already. Alignment and accountability count. I witnessed companies with such misalignment as to be paralyzed. They couldn't even decide on a strategic course of action that everyone could agree on. And I saw companies with such great alignment on great goals, with true accountability coursing through their workforce. I was involved with companies where honesty and integrity were in the corporate DNA and organizations without those critical traits. My pattern recognition was coming into focus, and every example drove home the potential power of my Leadership Principles, thus validating my own journey to them. My pattern recognition has been honed. I can see train wrecks coming today better than I ever could before. Pattern recognition is never 100 percent, but when your red flags go up, you better be prepared to get involved. I was formalizing my Leadership Principles and preparing a presentation appropriate for entrepreneurial groups and MBA programs.

Bonderman's Seventieth Birthday Party

DAVID BONDERMAN, JIM COULTER, AND Bill Price are the three cofounders of TPG. David was a fixture in Fort Worth, Texas, and was generally known as one of the smartest financial minds anywhere. I had heard of him for years, so I was excited to meet him as part of my recruitment into TPG. He was easy to talk to, and I quickly learned why everyone loved working with him. We had the opportunity to work together especially closely on the TXU Energy board. As a result of us spending so much time together and getting to know each other well, we even spent an afternoon at the University of Texas, where he was a distinguished guest at the McCombs School of Business. I was chairman of the McCombs Advisory Council at the time, and his presentation turned into a fireside chat spent in a Q&A session with me. I had submitted my questions to David in advance so I could ensure they would be fair game in front of a large audience. He called me and told me that wasn't any fun for him—he didn't want to know the questions in advance, and he was sure I would ask appropriate questions. He would look forward to some great back-and-forth. Vintage David Bonderman! That session couldn't have been more fun, and the audience greatly appreciated his candor!

For Bonderman's sixtieth birthday, he had arranged for the Rolling Stones to play for his private birthday party. That story grew over time: "Bondo," as most people who knew him referred to him, loved classic rock and roll. When Karleen and I got an invitation to Bondo's seventieth birthday party in 2012, it was an exciting day indeed! No one at TPG knew who the talent would be at his party, but there was high interest by everyone who was invited. His deal was that you had to get yourself to the Wynn Hotel in Las Vegas, and he would take care of everything else after that.

The stage was set, literally and figuratively. Secrecy surrounded the event. We needed multiple wristbands just to get to the part of the hotel where the event was to be held. There were more levels of security than you see with a presidential visit! They were determined to keep people out who were trying to crash his party. When we checked into the hotel, we got a box of treats that included an iPod Shuffle loaded with Bonderman's top five hundred favorite rock and roll songs and a printed sheet listing each song and artist in order.

At the appointed time we went to the ballroom where dinner was to be served. It was kind of a buffet setup, with lots of standing tables in front of a big stage and baseball bleachers at the back of the ballroom for those who were tired of standing. After some time for folks to meet, snack, and introduce each other—there were around four hundred people at the start of the evening—Bondo came out on stage to say hello and to thank everyone for coming. He said there would be a succession of acts, and he would introduce each act in turn. He wanted to first loosen up the group, and he succeeded when he announced his first act—Robin Williams. Williams did a one-hour set, which was spectacular, and, sure enough, everyone was positively giddy about how the evening had launched.

After another hour or more of eating and socializing, Bondo came back out to introduce the next act, John Fogerty and Creedence Clearwater Revival. I am a classic rock and roll nerd, and CCR has always been one of my favorite groups. I couldn't believe it. And they were fabulous, playing every one of their greatest hits and doing each one justice. The floor had been cleared, and it turned into a high school sock hop! So many guests were my vintage and shared my love for CCR, so everyone was dancing. Because I still hate to dance, I went up to the stage and just leaned on the stage and took it all in. Karleen, meanwhile, was dancing with her new friends. John Fogerty was five feet from me! I was transported back to my college days, with fond memories. When they finished the long set, there was another break. I noticed a lot of people wandering out, as it was getting very late and there had been plenty of food, drink, and dancing already. But Karleen and I stayed as we were, sure there was another act. Finally, with the clock close to midnight, the people remaining were told to move across the hall to a smaller venue for the last act.

The hundred or so people remaining walked across the hall and into a much more intimate setting, with tables, chairs, and a small bleacher section. The room could really only hold the people who were still there. When Bondo came out to introduce the last act, the room went dead silent. We all knew it must be someone really special, but no one could figure out who it might be. Bondo cleared that up quickly.

"Ladies and Gentlemen, Paul McCartney!"

Chills still run down my spine as I remember this. Karleen and I were maybe ten feet from Paul McCartney for two hours! He and his backups played all the greatest hits of the Beatles, complete with videos accompanying each hit. The rush of memories at a moment like that is hard to describe. I instantly remembered sitting on the floor in front of our black-and-white TV when I was twelve years old with my brothers and sister, watching Ed Sullivan introduce the Beatles, while my father muttered about their mop tops. The Beatles were my favorite group ever, and I think I knew all of their songs by heart. I grew up with them. When they went through their psychedelic phase I worried for them, and when Paul McCartney walked across Abbey Road barefoot, I wondered if he was indeed dead. I played their songs backward because I heard there were secrets to be found by playing the record backward. In short, I lived, ate, and drank the Beatles. And when John Lennon was shot, I went into shock and mourned along with my entire generation. Here Paul McCartney was—right in front of me. I couldn't really believe it. After each of his greatest songs, he chatted with people there. He had us all sing "Happy Birthday" to Bondo, which we all did, and then he told us stories from his Beatles days. I told Karleen we didn't need to attend another concert. Ever! We had been to the mountain. It was the most surreal evening ever.

Full Circle: Establishing a Mentoring Program at Texarkana Texas High School

AS I BEGAN THINKING ABOUT ways to give back after my Kinko's success, it felt good to focus my energies toward Texas High, my old high school. After all, Texas High in Texarkana had been so important in my life in many ways. I thought about how a) I didn't even know I was supposed to apply to a specific college and b) no one in the counseling office ever even asked if I wanted to talk about my college process. Without knowing the current state of college counseling at Texas High School, I began thinking about how I might put myself into a position to mentor the students with the highest potential at Texas High. Around 2006 all this led me to meet with Larry Sullivan, the superintendent of the Texarkana Independent School District, about formalizing a construct for putting me in front of ninth and tenth grade high-potential students to see if there was interest in building an ongoing relationship with me. I knew that while I wasn't in Ross Perot's league, I was a known entity in Texarkana and within Texas High School, so I was hopeful that some students would have interest.

It took one misfire to get the process headed in the right direction. I asked to meet with ten students with the highest potential, and the list they provided included photos and short bios. I believed the first set of students I saw fell far short of the type of students I was looking to meet. I just didn't feel that these kids were as aspirational as the students I envisioned working with. I sat down with the counselor and Texas High principal and wrote a description of the students I wanted to meet.

They needed to be:

1. At least top ten percent ranking, but hopefully top ten overall GPA. As I described to the counselor and principal, great grades are table stakes for getting accepted into great schools.
2. I wanted to see passion about something, and it didn't really matter what it was. It just needed to be something that could become a college essay.
3. The person could be lopsided instead of well rounded. It would make them more interesting than a student who just checked a bunch of boxes.
4. I wanted students who were open and honest in their communications: kids who owned their shortcomings as well as their strengths.

It was amazing, as if a light went on for both the counselor and the principal. They both said they now understood, and if I could give them a bit of time, they would introduce me to a completely different set of students.

And that began my fifteen-year odyssey with Texas High students, which ended in 2021. It ended due to a combination of factors, including losing the face-to-face aspect of it because of COVID. Since I had a two-year hiatus, I also realized that the process was becoming a bit forced for me, so I decided to stick a pin into that specific work and declare victory. To jump forward to today:

1. There is an entire wall where the school tacks names of seniors and the college they decided to attend.
2. Students today go to outstanding colleges all over America, including Ivy League schools, Duke, Northwestern, Stanford, Notre Dame, and all the military academies. And the students attend so many different schools, with greater numbers of students matriculating in faraway places than ever before.
3. The school tracks and publishes the amount of scholarship dollars in total that is spread among seniors headed to colleges. The total scholarship dollars that THS students received in 2006 was about $3.5 million, and by 2021 it was about $17.5 million.

In short, there is an ecosystem at the school today that promotes reaching higher and further to all its students.

While my conversations with students have always been confidential, I can share a few stories that I feel best represent the kind of stories I heard and issues some students faced.

My first meeting with the first batch of students who fit the new description was exciting. The students sat around a long table and all seemed curious about me and what I was doing in that room talking to them. The table had a real mishmash of students: all shapes, sizes, and colors, and equal numbers of each gender. I loved it! I looked around, trying to determine the first person I should engage with. I randomly picked a young girl at the far end of the table. I asked her to tell me about herself, and she pretty much gave just the obvious specifics: top ten ranking, some AP courses, and would be editor of the school newspaper the next year. I call that name, rank, and serial number! Next, I asked her what she did outside of class. She told me she had just gotten her first black belt in Tae Kwon Do, and she was the youngest and first female Tae Kwon Do referee in America. Bingo! What a perfect candidate for what I envisioned. I asked her about her personal life. It turns out her family had come from Mexico, and they lived with relatives in Eagle Pass, Texas. Because her grades were so strong, her parents sent her to Texarkana to live with her grandparents to get a better education than she might in Eagle Pass. When I moved on to what she wanted to be in the future, she relayed that she wanted to be an architect and specialize in building durable homes for lower-income groups of people. She said that a tornado had hit Eagle Pass a few years prior, and the lower-income homes were mostly destroyed, while most of the middle- and high-income homes had withstood the storm. That didn't sit well with her. I, of course, was overjoyed at her aspirations. I wanted to pay it forward at Texas High, and the first person I chatted with was exactly the kind of person who I wanted to help. I paid for her grandparents to bring her to Dallas and meet with Bruce Bernbaum, the senior partner at Bernbaum-Magadini architectural firm, to show her what her life as an architect might look like and also to discuss her idea about building stronger homes in lower-income areas. The University of Texas architecture school accepted her for admission, but, as it worked out, the University of Arkansas offered her a free six-year education to go to Fayetteville for college, and that's where she went.

Another young man once sent me an email that read as follows: "I would like to be a chemical engineer. Can you tell me what a chemical engineer does?" Think about that for a second! I was so excited to work with him that I called Walter Levy, the CEO of NCH, a global company in the business of cleaning water, conserving energy, and delivering maintenance solutions, based in Dallas. I told Walter what I was trying to do, and he jumped to help. He planned a day when our young Texas High student could travel with an NCH water engineer on his route in East Texas. And then Walter also planned a day in Dallas when the student could visit the corporate offices and be shown the various activities that chemical engineers engage in daily.

The way it worked out over time was that I would start with ten to twelve ninth and tenth graders. They all would engage for a while, and then some would fall off. Usually, three to four students in each cohort stay fully engaged through twelfth grade and beyond. For these three to four students, I would spend a lot of time talking with them about admissions processes and helping them think about essays that would catch the attention of college admissions readers. I was known as the guy who many times wrote "So what?" or "Who cares?" in the margins of their essays to give tough love, helping them achieve their admissions goals.

One of my more satisfying moments was when a father brought his son to Dallas for a breakfast so we could further discuss my comments on his son's college essay. The student had thought it was a particularly fine essay and wanted to be sure he understood my comments. As we were talking during that breakfast, the father elbowed his son and gently told him that he might want to tell me what was really bothering him. With that, the son began to talk about how he had been an only child and his parents had recently adopted a child and it had upended his home life and his relationship with his parents. I said that was *exactly* what an admissions reader would want to hear to better understand who he was and the how and why of the impact it had on him. His father smiled broadly. The son looked at me and said he was shocked to hear anyone might want to read about that but that he would think about it. He did change his essay, and he did get into his first choice.

I have followed several of "my" kids into their thirties, along with many still in their twenties. Karleen and I have been invited to weddings, and I have surprised many at their colleges. It has been very gratifying and scratches my itch to see firsthand how giving back has helped students reach higher and further. And each successful outcome takes me back to that May evening in 1969, when I sat in that chair next to Ross Perot and first engaged with him, changing my life.

Breaking Down My Evolution over a Long Career

WHAT A SAGA MY CAREER has been! Part of my learning process has always been to try to create order from what appears at the outset to be chaos. From my vantage point today, it feels easier to plot a progression of my career than it might have felt in the midst of it. Reflecting upon my personal journey from a small-town child who kept his own counsel as he viewed the world around him to the person I am today, I feel I have teased out the evolution of my own life through seven discrete steps:

1. Curiosity
2. Gaining Experiences
3. Pattern Recognition
4. Tactical Decision Rules
5. Strategic Leadership Principles
6. Culture Building
7. Paying It Forward (mentoring, storytelling, and teaching)

The reason I created this list—besides that it appeals to my analytical side and gives me comfort that my career had a beginning, middle, and end—is primarily so I have a construct to show mentees when I begin to hear their issues revolving around where they are in their careers. If I am mentoring someone in their early career, I try to help them give themselves permission to not have a big success just yet.

This also works for people in different stages and ages. I do firmly believe that everyone views their world through a unique prism. While my seven steps likely won't work for others in the exact way I have laid them out for myself, each person can construct a list from their own journey. It may have three steps instead of seven, or even ten steps, but it helps to have a process with which to evaluate our journeys. There is often something very important to take away from an exercise like this. It can even inform a person what makes the most sense for them as the next steps in their journey.

With that background, I will expand a bit on the steps of my personal evolution.

1. Curiosity

That I kept my own counsel as a young child was simply because I had no adult to talk with about questions that swirled in my head. I was a curious child, and my curiosity has lasted a lifetime. It's why I love learning, and that has stayed with me. And it's also why I so love the saying "Don't confuse a flash of insight for the light of truth." Just because I had an insight about something I had been pondering, followed by an "aha!" moment, it didn't necessarily mean my insight was true or correct. I began considering those insights as breakthrough thoughts that needed pressure testing. And I learned that it is not a process for one person playing mind games by himself. The best way to get to truth is to collaborate, to take in other people's points of view. And that is where the Socratic approach was so helpful for me. The fact is that there are often many equally good truths. And while this was especially important to me, it also helped in other ways.

2. Gaining Experiences

I feel that I had to grow through each step to truly appreciate and understand my journey. I do think the array of experiences I had when I was young and impressionable provided the fodder for my curiosity and began coloring my worldview. In my mind I was filing everything happening to me away, from watching the indignities doled out to my coworkers and friends in the furniture warehouse simply because of their skin color to the experience of flying with a billionaire, proximity to rock stars and other celebrities, and feeling the brunt of corporate politics swatting at me. All these experiences and so many more were critical to my growth. Especially when a person is young, every experience feels like a life changer. Some indeed may be, but the excitement of youth leads to lifelong memories that grow larger with time.

3. Pattern Recognition

Because vivid experiences are burned into the brain while it is so impressionable, there is a real opportunity to find threads of similarity amongst very dissimilar events. Patterns emerge in benign experiences like seeing the pattern of what happens when bad behavior as a child gets out of control in school or at home. And patterns are apparent in more nuanced situations, such as peeling back disparate behaviors in disparate situations and learning that there are many people motivated by self-interest or greed. Patterns begin to pop up in so many places and in so many ways, and, with practice over time, the ability to discern a pattern becomes easier and easier, especially as one gets older and more experienced.

4. Tactical Decision Rules

Corporate decisions begin having more far-reaching implications as one moves up the corporate ladder, and so do the issues that surface when increased collaboration is built into decision making. These decision rules typically apply to operational issues, and as you deal more with peers at the top of the corporate organization, self-interest increasingly becomes a key driver of behaviors. A drive for either more personal power or greater compensation in the workplace tends to lead to the types of issues that often rear their head at the top of an organization chart. And in the heat of the moment, during a session meant to be collaborative, sometimes people don't think as clearly as they should.

I developed sets of decision rules that were easier to gain agreement with across a group in the cool light of morning rather than in the heat of battle. The tactical decision rules could apply in areas like discount charts that clearly define how discounts are earned by customers. They can also be used to establish elements like various thresholds for incentive compensation and what will be the most important weighted filters when evaluating people's performance for compensation and promotions. Again, decision rules are installed mainly to give process to those issues that people sometimes tend to think about through a filter of their own career needs instead of the common good of the company.

5. Strategic Leadership Principles

These are the behaviors that define how companies engage with and are received by their team members, customers, suppliers, investors, and the communities in which they operate. Decision rules tend to deal with tactical issues, while leadership principles tend to deal with strategic, core corporate DNA behaviors. They primarily lay out what the company will stand for, what it wants to be known for, and what behaviors will be rewarded. Implicit in a good set of leadership principles is the notion that behaviors that are opposed to a leadership principle will not be accepted and will be dealt with clearly and quickly. There is not one definitive set of leadership principles: there can be many, just as the Socratic teaching method illustrated so long ago. My personal Leadership Principles will follow this section.

6. Culture Building

I also believe that you simply can't legislate a corporate culture. A corporate culture is the *result* of leadership principles that are core to the company and inform corporate behaviors in the marketplace and the way a company treats its team members and customers. It is the icing on a corporate cake. If the cake is made well, it becomes a thing of beauty. If the cake is not made well, then the corporate culture is in fact hollow. A strong set of Leadership Principles is critical, and it can, in fact, stand the test of time. When there is a strong set of Leadership Principles, other very positive things come to life inside the company, and those things become proxies for a strong set of Leadership Principles. A strong example is something that Paul Orfalea installed at Kinko's. Let's say a team member named Bertha Kirkpatrick was head of the mail room, which means she was in charge of disseminating information to twelve hundred separate stores and fielding all the questions that stores might have about communication topics. Now suppose Bertha had an idea for a digital newsletter that each store received on Mondays that not only laid out big topics for that week but also provided a calendar of new initiatives coming down over the next month. With this information, individual stores could better plan and staff for coming events. In the world of Kinko's, that newsletter would become a reality, and the title of the newsletter would be *The Bertha Kirkpatrick Weekly Information Newsletter.* Guess what happens to Bertha for the rest of her career at Kinko's? When she calls anyone in a store or meets anyone at a company event and says her name is Bertha Kirkpatrick, people step back and say something like, "Wow, you are *the* Bertha Kirkpatrick? Incredible! Can I take a photo with you? Hey Sofia, get over here. This is Bertha Kirkpatrick!" And on and on. Not only does Bertha feel seen and appreciated, but the company team members have a clear example of the appreciation and respect Kinko's has for its team members. Each year at its annual convention, Kinko's would announce top new initiatives by team members, along with the name of the new idea, which always incorporated the name of the person who conceived the idea.

One more incredible idea from Kinko's. The stores couldn't afford to have janitorial services come in to clean the restrooms, so the rule was the newest employee had to clean restrooms until the next new employee showed up. And guess what? If you were a new store manager who got promoted and moved to a different Kinko's store, *you* had to clean the restrooms as anyone else would until there was a newer team member than you!

Those are examples of outputs from a healthy culture where the team members felt heard and that they were part of a team, all buying into a corporate vision.

7. Paying It Forward
(Mentoring, Storytelling, and Teaching)

I suppose this is a bit like the saying "To a carpenter with a hammer, everything looks like a nail," but I do believe that mentoring, storytelling, and teaching are incumbent on anyone who has had a successful career in any sector. We all learn what we learn, but some of us take a longer time and a more circuitous path than others. I am certainly one of those people. But as a tip of the hat to the next generation in whatever space you are in, why wouldn't you pay it forward? Everyone is different, but I have always felt that if I can level the playing field for people younger than I am, that is a double win. So that's what I do. But no matter how you do what you do, paying it forward is a great thing.

As promised, my Leadership Principles.

Kusin Leadership Principles

THERE IS NO CLEAR DELINEATION point when I announced my Leadership Principles for the first time. They grew organically out of my experiences at the myriad of businesses preceding Kinko's. In addition to the extraordinary leadership skills to which I had been exposed from so many great team members, colleagues, and mentors, I had also seen some pretty horrific examples of malignant leadership. I developed the point of view that teams really do draw their energy and habits from their leaders and the leadership skills their leaders embrace. Great leaders, in addition to being able to paint an aspirational picture of a flag on a distant hill, must clearly lay out what behaviors the team should embody. If a leader cuts corners or makes decisions that reflect greed or a power grab, the teams they lead will assume those are righteous behaviors and emulate them to the detriment of their organization.

Somewhere along the way, I limited my list of Leadership Principles to five. A number that is five or a multiple of five is well understood. But due to writing this book I have thought more deeply about my experiences from a different vantage point. I've realized that I actually have always had six Leadership Principles, though I usually talked about only five for the reason above, and I've tossed around a couple of the principles over the years to see which fit the best. I am throwing that thinking out, given how the world has changed in the last ten or so years, and I'm sticking with all six of my Leadership Principles.

These six Leadership Principles serve as my North Star in business. Ever since Kinko's, where I first publicly verbalized them, I always discuss the following principles, fleshing each out a bit. Here are my six Leadership Principles.

1. Alignment

The entire team needs to agree on the organization's goals and objectives and internalize them at the individual team member level. Passive-aggressive behaviors are poison to any company. Nodding yes in a meeting and then trashing what was said afterward is passive-aggressive poison. I have always thought that every company needs its own Darth Vader competitor. While it is fun to compete against a natural rival, it is more important for each team member to embrace the company's most noble objectives and take them as their own.

2. Respect for Others

TPG had a sign in its lobby: "NO ASSHOLES ALLOWED." While some people laughed and others were offended, the message was clear and regularly enforced. The private equity industry is known for having some bad actors. Those behaviors were not going to be allowed at TPG, and I appreciated it. I have met too many toxic people in my career to want to be involved with such individuals ever again. Going all the way back to my teenage, furniture delivery years, lack of respect has chilled me at my core. No one deserves to be disrespected, ever. Yet in the world we live in today a complete lack of civility has become part of our nation's narrative. This is very easy for anyone in any company to understand. TPG had it right in their lobby!

3. **Accountability**

    Every team member needs to be very clear on exactly what
    they are accountable for, and in return the company needs
    to ensure that each team member has the appropriate tools
    necessary to deliver against their accountabilities. Proper tool
    kits include full responsibility for results, authority to do what
    is needed to achieve their accountability, and the full backing
    of their bosses up the chain of command. I get very frustrated
    when there is accountability without either responsibility or
    authority. I have been amazed in my career at the number
    of people who failed, not due to any shortcomings of their
    own, but rather because they were not given adequate
    tools, responsibility, or authority to achieve their specific
    accountabilities. Companies that do not give authority to
    match responsibility ultimately develop malignant cultures.

4. **Open and Honest Communications**

    Say what you mean, and mean what you say. Many times
    I have told teams, just as Jack Welch told me, that no one
    should ever, ever be surprised if they are fired. Interactions
    between team members need to be open and honest. If a
    team member doesn't believe in an aspirational goal, it's
    incumbent on them to raise their hand and express their
    issues in an open way. Conversely, when corporate leaders are
    open about their shortcomings and failures, it breeds trust in
    their organization and a greater likelihood that their team
    members will be open and honest with their own teams.

5. **Honesty and Integrity**

    We work for our customers, our team members, our suppliers,
    our investors, and the communities in which we operate. We
    owe it to each of our constituencies to be above reproach in
    all of our dealings, all of the time. It is always best to tell

the truth, if for no other reason than that you never have to remember what you said to someone. And frankly, after being part of a very high-integrity team at Babbage's, I had a couple of bad experiences prior to Kinko's, where I saw firsthand the damage that can be caused by a lack of honesty and integrity. And I think you have to see bad to properly understand good.

6. **Continuous Improvement**

I am at my jumpiest when business is good. I know that it's usually impossible to see around corners and that bad stuff always happens. I also know that it is a bit of a human reflex to relax when things are going very well. That makes me crazy—we must always think about how we can do whatever it is that we do better, smarter, and faster than we have before. Constant improvement is not an annual exercise. It should be an everyday thing and permeate everything that happens in a company. As I related earlier, if there is one thing Jim and I missed at Babbage's, which would have made a ton of difference, it was the requirement for continuous improvement. We didn't understand properly the power of that principle.

It's important to note that there is no single set of Leadership Principles that might trump all others. Each person's individual prism will accent different traits and characteristics. One thing is true, not just in corporations but in general for everyone in a society: people want and need those in power to model strong principles. Every person can develop their own principles, and I absolutely support that!

Key Lessons

PART 7

Embrace Strategic Partnerships:
Seek partnerships that create mutual benefits and amplify success, like the symbiotic relationship between FedEx and Kinko's.

Navigate High-Stakes Negotiations:
When opportunities like the FedEx acquisition arise, negotiate with confidence, clarity, and an understanding of your business's value.

Leverage Company Strengths:
Understand and utilize your company's unique strengths, as exemplified by Kinko's high-traffic stores for FedEx.

Prepare for Unforeseen Opportunities:
Always be ready for the unexpected, and don't be afraid to engage in discussions that could lead to transformative outcomes.

Lead with a Balanced Approach:
Combine a strong work ethic with empathy and understanding, drawing on experiences like those at Kinko's, when respecting the team was paramount.

Recognize and Cultivate Talent:
Acknowledge the potential in your team members and foster their growth, just as many Kinko's employees became successful CEOs.

Share Success with the Team:
Celebrate victories with your team, showing gratitude
in ways like the custom boots after the Kinko's sale,
reinforcing a collective achievement.

Value Relationships and Bonds:
Prioritize and cherish the connections you make, much like
the bond formed between myself and Fred Smith, for long-
term personal and professional fulfillment.

Embrace Continuous Learning:
Whether it's understanding FedEx's package margin strategies
or entering private equity, maintain a learner's mindset.

Assess Career Transitions:
When considering moves like the switch to private equity,
align them with your passion for learning and pattern
recognition skills.

Immerse Yourself in New Industries with Curiosity:
Use your experience to contribute to diverse fields, similar
to the engagement with companies like Petco and TXU
Energy at TPG.

Formulate Leadership Principles:
Develop a personal code of leadership principles that reflect
your experiences and insights, just as the Kusin Leadership
Principles were established.

Give Back and Mentor Others:
Take the initiative to mentor and guide the next generation,
drawing on your journey to help others find their path, as
I did with Texarkana Texas High School students.

Pride and Gratitude

IT HAS GIVEN ME GREAT pride to reflect back on the companies I have cofounded and those I joined as CEO or as an adviser. I still love the department-store business and remain dear friends with Marvin Goldstein, my first and greatest business mentor at the Emporium, who is now retired and plays golf in Palm Springs with his wife Harriet in the winters and in Minneapolis during the summers. I speak to him often and have loved our relationship, which has now spanned many of our families' life events. Terry Lundgren spent his career in department stores and masterfully turned Macy's around to create the national footprint for the top-tier department store in America. He and his super wife Tina remain close and dear friends.

Jim McCurry and I share the joint pride of having cofounded Babbage's and growing it through its first thirteen to fifteen years of growth and evolution into GameStop. There has been quite a ride for GameStop since, as it has negotiated the major product life cycles and evolution of the video game industry for decades. We are so proud to have opened the world's first video game store at a time when the general population had no idea what the word *software* even meant. I still marvel that the inventory management software we developed when our earliest software crashed in our third year continued to be used by GameStop for decades. Jim and his wife, Peggy, now split their time between Asheville, North Carolina, and Amelia Island in Florida. Jim and I speak regularly and play golf annually at our HBS Section H golf outing.

I'm also very pleased that my thinking through the evolution of the cosmetics industry led me to realize that the cyclical nature of that industry was about to create new opportunities for makeup artist brands. This led to me recruiting Janet Gurwitch and cofounding and launching an early makeup artist concept. We launched the Laura Mercier brand and did well enough that I could hand the company off completely to her several years later and allow her to push it to great heights with her crack team.

But Kinko's was my baby, and it gave me the opportunity to take all that I had learned to build a world-class team, achieve an unprecedented turnaround, and successfully sell the company to FedEx. Dan Connors and I have remained very close friends. He has enjoyed his business life after Kinko's, stepping into several troubled companies, turning each around, building value along the way, and then successfully selling each. He certainly did that for Kinko's. And he has traded in his "high and tight" haircuts for flowing shoulder-length hair and is quite the fashion plate these days. Who knew that back then Dan had completely hidden his GQ tendencies from the Bain cultural norms! He and his wife, Shannon, have enjoyed building new homes in each city where he has worked. I particularly love the photos he shares of himself backstage with Keith Richards. Or was it Paul McCartney, with Dan wearing his finest bright-red sport coat? Or was it both? Dan may love classic rock and roll more than I do, or at least he's enjoying it more! But his real love is Notre Dame football, and he has been deeply involved in that university over many, many years.

TPG has changed pretty dramatically in the years since I left. It had been very much a family business, with the cofounders involved in all aspects of the firm's operations, but it had to become more corporate as it moved toward becoming a public company. Those things have to happen sometimes, but it lost many of its early veterans like Carrie Wheeler, Tim Dunn, and Dick Boyce, whom I worked with all along the way.

My mentoring activities remain robust, but I intentionally leave blocks of my time open for my family. All of our four kids now have families of their own, so I now have a combined eight kids (I claim our original four plus their spouses as our own these days!), all leading such interesting lives. Most are entrepreneurial in their own right, self-starters who excel in their chosen fields. And I am a beneficiary, getting to learn from each of them as they traverse their careers. The most important thing I have learned is that I must be available when the phone rings, or I miss an opportunity. If I have to ask if I can call them later that day or the next, there's a high likelihood that they will get their mentoring needs filled elsewhere. When that happens, I consider it a failure on my part.

Opportunities to learn and teach seem to find me on a regular basis. Recently, in the space of only a couple of hours, I was able to help extended family members think through issues unique to their journeys. One was questioning the advisability of jumping to a new company with a better compensation package versus staying in a position he enjoyed with great upside for him, but with less compensation. He was also considering that he has a personal debt load he worries about. All I did was ask a series of questions based on how he answered my prior question, and within thirty minutes he arrived at his own answer and felt great about it. He hurried off to set his plan into motion. The other family member was loving his job working at a private school and had been thinking about how he could help the school by adding a finer point to its mission statement that related to his particular work area. By the time we finished chatting, he had a plan and was very pleased and eager to start putting it into motion. All I had done with both these folks was simply to ask questions. Even today, years after Dan Connors and I are no longer working together, I frequently use Dan's words, "I might invite you to think about _____." Not pushy, not aggressive, and not taking power from the person I'm speaking with, just inviting them to perhaps think a bit differently.

I likely still have at least fifty mentoring sessions a year of one type or another. And I recently launched a podcast on mentoring, cohosting with my longtime friend Jill Louis. It is such a win-win for me. I *love* when I see lights go on in someone's eyes as they have their own moment of sudden, triumphant discovery, inspiration, or insight. And I most love when it feels like I'm leveling the playing field for someone. That is the highest value add for me. It really fills me up.

I used to tease Karleen that she could start crying during a thirty-second commercial. Today I realize that the place Karleen comes from is always love and gratitude. She put on a clinic raising our four kids. I was around as much as I could be, but I recognize that Karleen was the glue holding our family together. She remains a role model to our larger extended family, providing unconditional love for all the generations. She is a force of nature in parenting and grandparenting. Not only has she done an incredible job with our children and grandchildren, she has been such a role model for me and given me permission to work on myself. She showed incredible patience with my fits and starts as a husband and a father. Today my grandkids crawl all over me and love me as a big tease who is full of love for each of them, but when something happens and they need hugs and consoling, it isn't me they run toward!

My life is so full, and I'm specifically so full of gratitude for the quality of the journey I've had. When I see a person getting a dose of love or having their playing field leveled up to others who may have had more advantages, I do cry from happiness for them. And now it's me who is teased when I cry during a thirty-second commercial. To quote the Grateful Dead, "What a long, strange trip it's been!"

ACKNOWLEDGMENTS

I'VE ALWAYS BREEZED RIGHT PAST acknowledgments when reading a new book. Never again! I couldn't possibly have predicted the lengths I would go to to confirm the facts of my stories, nor could I have known how eager people would be to help where they could. I would like to seriously acknowledge the people who were so mission critical to creating this book. It wouldn't exist without them all!

I met Maria Gagliano after a long search for an editor, working my way through many author referrals, websites, and finally conducting Zoom interviews. A book industry veteran, Maria is not only a book pro, she also was a super therapist. She challenged my thinking and my personal narrative and ultimately got me to believe that perhaps there was more intention than serendipity in my career. That thought changed how I thought about my stories and my lessons. She is world class in every way, and this book wouldn't be this book without her invisible hand! In addition, as I was such an amateur in the book industry, Maria took on the additional role of sherpa, guiding me through the book industry. I shouldn't be surprised that Maria would assemble a team of equally outstanding book professionals. Beth Blachman did an outstanding job on copyediting, making me sound way smarter than I am, and Zoe Norvell so creatively designed the cover and the interiors of the book. Dan Avant was such a terrific and meticulous proofreader. Finally, Joe Scalora coached me and directed me in producing the audiobook version of the book. Maria is so strong in everything she has done to help me get this book out into the wild. Thank you, Maria!

I enjoyed reconnecting with so many team members from my past. I had thorough conversations with Marvin Goldstein and Walter Gerken from my department-store days, rehashing those crazy and fun years. Memories also flooded back about my Babbage's years from conversations with Jim McCurry, Opal Ferraro, Mary Rummelhart, and Terri Yerant, along with a fabulous two-hour lunch with Ron Freeman! Dan Connors filled in so many blanks for me when we caught up on several occasions. Paul Rostron and I compared notes over lunch, confirming our memories about the events of September 11, 2001, when Kinko's was heavily involved with the FBI in establishing who were the terrorists that tragic day.

Of course, my family! I felt the love from all eight of my children, each in their own unique ways. Ben Kusin and Marina Monroe, Caroline Kusin Pritchard and Tavita Pritchard, Eric and Irene Kusin, and Elizabeth Kusin Vivero and David Vivero—thank you all for the help, support, and love you have shown me during the process. They kept me in the middle of the road, refusing to let me careen from guardrail to guardrail, as I often do. And they were really cheering on Maria, who they couldn't believe was so effective at managing me! Finally, Karleen had the final word on everything, though always in her own unique way. I loved how she would read a manuscript, think for a while, and then, in her own way, move me around to different words or a different thought. As always, she was spot-on with all her callouts!

ABOUT THE AUTHOR

GARY KUSIN is a mentor, investor, entrepreneur, and business adviser. Gary cofounded two companies: Babbage's, operating today as GameStop (NYSE: GME), and Laura Mercier Cosmetics, both of which today are well-known global brands. Gary spent thirteen years as a senior adviser to the global private equity firm TPG, including a large amount of his time mentoring CEOs of TPG portfolio companies. He served from 2001–2006 as president and chief executive officer of Kinko's, today operating as FedEx Office. Gary was responsible for the turnaround, strategic growth, and transformation of Kinko's and oversaw the ultimate sale to FedEx, directly reporting to Fred Smith, founder of FedEx, for the two years required to integrate Kinko's into FedEx and be renamed FedEx Office. He today advises an array of public and private companies, large and small, on strategy, management, and growth issues. In addition, Gary continues his full schedule of mentoring and has mentored well over a thousand individuals during the course of his career.

An *Inc.* magazine "Entrepreneur of the Year," he has served on many public and private boards of directors for firms both in America and abroad, including names such as Electronic Arts, Petco, Sabre, and Myer Department Stores in Australia.

Gary has been very involved in Dallas community activities throughout his career. A representative sample of organizations and positions includes the St. Mark's School of Texas Board of Trustees, Dallas Young Presidents' Organization (YPO) chairman, Dallas Citizen's Council board of directors, and the Southwestern Medical School Foundation.

A member of the University of Texas McCombs School of Business Hall of Fame, Gary earned a BA from the University of Texas at Austin and an MBA from Harvard Business School. A native of Texarkana, Texas, Gary lives in Dallas with his wife, Karleen. Their four children, their children's spouses, and their eleven grandchildren live from coast to coast, and most of them are on their own entrepreneurial journeys.